ESSENTIAL
CYPRUS

★ Best places to see 34–55

▮ Featured sight

Original text by Robert Bulmer

Updated by Lara Dunston

© Automobile Association Developments Limited 2009
First published 2007
Reprinted 2009. Information verified and updated

ISBN: 978-0-7495-6007-2

Published by AA Publishing, a trading name of Automobile Association Developments
Limited, whose registered office is Fanum House, Basing View, Basingstoke,
Hampshire RG21 4EA.Registered number 1878835.

Automobile Association Developments Limited retains the copyright in the original
edition © 1998 and in all subsequent editions, reprints and amendments

A CIP catalogue record for this book is available from the British Library

Colour separation: MRM Graphics Ltd
Printed and bound in Italy by Printer Trento S.r.l.

A03616
Maps in this title produced from mapping © Freytag-Berndt u. Artaria KG,
1231 Vienna-Austria
with additional information from Cyprus Tourism Organisation © State Copyright
reserved and Turkish Republic of Northern Cyprus tourist office

About this book

This book is divided into five sections.

The essence of Cyprus pages 6–19
Introduction; Features; Food and drink; Short break including the 10 Essentials

Planning pages 20–33
Before you go; Getting there; Getting around; Being there

Best places to see pages 34–55
The unmissable highlights of any visit to Cyprus

Best things to do pages 56–81
Great places to have lunch; activities; beaches; places to take the children; off the beaten track; best views and more

Exploring pages 82–186
The best places to visit in Cyprus, organized by area

Maps All map references are to the maps on the covers. For example, Nicosia has the reference 🕂 16J – indicating the grid square in which it can be found.

Admission prices
Inexpensive (under €2.50/YTL4.75); Moderate (€2.50/YTL4.75–€5/YTL9.50); Expensive (over €5/YTL9.50)

Hotel prices Room per night (Republic of Cyprus/North Cyprus): € budget (under €60/YTL115); €€ moderate (€60–€120/YTL115–YTL230); €€ expensive to luxury (over €120/YTL230)

Restaurant prices A 3-course meal per person without drinks (Republic of Cyprus/North Cyprus): € budget (under €40/YTL77); €€ moderate (€40–€60/YTL77–YTL115); €€€ expensive (over €60/YTL115)

Contents

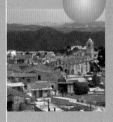

The essence of...

Cyprus is a land of contour and light – hills, valleys and plains. There are beaches, although not endless sands. The heat of summer robs the land of life: winter rains restore spectacular colour. With its archaeological wonders Cyprus is certainly the stuff of tourist books.

But what of the less tangible Cyprus? There is the interesting first journey to the hotel, with screeching brakes and tyres. Less disconcerting are the marvellous alfresco gastronomic events under awnings at lunch-time and the stars at night. Walks through the pine forests of the high mountains, with their magnificent views, will long be remembered.

features

Cyprus, within sight of Asia Minor, is halfway to the Orient, yet it looks more and more to the west. The majority of its visitors are from Europe and in 2004 it joined the European Union. English is spoken island-wide, a legacy of British colonial rule. Nevertheless, in many respects Cyprus remains different and retains its own culture. This complex mixture stems from its location and history. Over the centuries Cyprus has been controlled by most great Mediterranean powers and its people have a diverse, if not exotic, ancestry.

The separation of the island today is an indirect consequence of the arrival of the Ottoman Turks in the 16th century. It is not a division easily ignored – United Nations soldiers and Greek and Turkish flags are everywhere along the Green Line. Nevertheless few visitors dwell on the political situation. Understandably they have other distractions.

GEOGRAPHY

● The island has two significant mountain ranges. Troodos in the centre reaches 1,951m (6,401ft), high enough to ensure snow cover in winter; the Pentadaktylos (Beşparmak) Mountains at 1,046m (3,431ft), are in the Turkish controlled district.

● There are approximately 3,350 hours of sunshine a year, with little chance of rain between May and October.

● The sheep cope with the shortage of grazing in the dry summer by storing fat in their tails.

POPULATION

● The first sign of human habitation dates from 11,000 years ago.

● The island's population is estimated at 985,000, of whom about 640,000 are Greek Cypriots, 180,000 Turkish Cypriots, 8,000 Armenians and Maronites, and the rest foreign residents.

● Cypriots have the highest marriage rate in Europe.

ECONOMIC FACTORS

● Forty-six per cent of the land area is cultivated; the main crops are cereals, potatoes and citrus fruits.

● Cyprus has a standard of living slightly higher than the EU average.

● Cyprus has suffered water shortages because of dry winters. As a result, three desalination plants have been constructed off the south coast and a fourth off the east, providing 120,000cu m (26.4 million gallons) of water per day.

TOURISM

● The island attracts about 2.49 million visitors a year and tourism provides employment for around 113,000 people or 30 per cent of the work force, many of them immigrants.

food & drink

Cyprus has plenty of fresh produce and meat, and visitors should take the opportunity to make the most of the fruits that are so plentiful in the summer months. Quite apart from the well-known crops of citrus fruits, there are peaches, plums, cherries, melons and bananas – all readily available in season. Watermelons and other fruits are often sold from roadside stalls.

GREEK CUISINE

The old staples of Greek cuisine – moussaka, *stifado*, kebab and Greek salad – will be much in evidence. The *meze* is perhaps a good way to get an insight into Cypriot food. *Meze*, or *mezedhes*, is a series of small different dishes that are provided throughout an evening, and may cover absolutely everything or pursue a fish or a meat theme. In a good restaurant the *meze* can contain up to 30 different dishes and it is important to pace yourself through the meal.

Kebab *(souvlaki)* appears on all menus, and lamb is another common dish, either lamb chops or the more traditional *kleftiko*, which consists of large

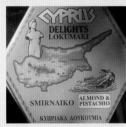

pieces of lamb baked slowly in traditional *kleftiko* ovens. Cypriots also have a taste for smoked meats, most notably the traditional *loukanika* sausage.

Fish is expensive, although *kalamari* – squid cooked in batter – is good value and widely available. Other fish options include swordfish, red mullet (*barbouni* in Greek), whitebait and sea bass. Alternatively, fresh farmed trout is on the menu in some of the mountain villages.

Halloumi cheese is the main dairy product distinctive to the island. It is made from goat's milk and is often served grilled. The cheese is available in most supermarkets.

Visitors should seek out some of the cake shops that attract local custom. The traditional Greek desserts such as *baklava* and *cadefi* may be too sweet for some tastes,

but the wide range of custard-based cakes should appeal to all, as will the biscuits, which can be bought by weight in these shops.

A similar range of food is available in the Turkish part of the island. Some dishes such as *sis kebab* and *cacik* (cucumber and yoghurt salad) will already be familiar, but there are many other delights, among them *elma dizmesi*, a dish of apple and meat patties, and *cuvecte yaz turlusu*, a tasty summer stew.

WINE, BRANDY AND BEER

Cypriot wine is plentiful and inexpensive, and it is claimed that it has been made in Cyprus since 2000BC. The main wineries are at Limassol, but, increasingly, smaller producers are developing and some of the villages and monasteries now produce their own wines. It is an important business that is now worth €20 million a year in exports.

Commandaria sweet wine is one of Cyprus's best known wines and it is said that it was drunk during the ancient festivals of Aphrodite. However, its origins can only be definitively traced back to the estate of the Knights Hospitaller at Kolossi, 700 years ago.

The island's brandy can no longer be labelled as such because of an EU directive that insists on a 36 per cent alcohol content. But, with lemons and angostura bitters it still makes fabulous brandy sours. Keo and Carlsberg beers are among those brewed locally.

short break

If you have only a short time to visit Cyprus and would like to take home some unforgettable memories you can do something local and capture the real flavour of the island. The following suggestions will give you a wide range of sights and experiences that won't take very long, won't cost very much and will make your visit very special. If you only have time to choose just one of these, you will have found the true heart of Cyprus.

● **Go to the Roman theatre at Kourion**
(► 42–43) for classical drama: the atmosphere is electric. Performances are held throughout the year (details from the tourist office).

● **Find a quiet beach,** preferably fringed with bushes or tall grasses, and take a swim long before breakfast.

● **Have a drink in a village coffee shop.** Be prepared to be ignored, but it is much more likely that someone will chance their English and start a conversation.

● **Join a plate-breaking session in a Greek taverna.** This mayhem is not as common as it once was, but enquiries may lead to a venue.

● **Get invited to a village wedding,** witness the chaotic church service and drink and eat all night under the stars.

● **Ski or toboggan on Mount Olympos** (➤ 154–155). No chance here for summer visitors – the season is from December or January to early March.

● **Have a full alfresco *meze* off the tourist track,** but be prepared to stay awake all night with a distended stomach.

● **Drive to Petra tou Romiou,** or the Rock of Romios – better known as the Rock of Aphrodite (➤ 113) – in the late afternoon and stop on the clifftop a little to the east. The view is spectacular.

● **Join in a Greek dance.** The impressiveness of the steps is hardly matched by the difficulty. Have a couple of brandy sours first.

● **Walk a forest trail in the Troodos or Pentadaktylos mountains** until perspiring freely, then sit down and enjoy a picnic.

Planning

Before you go

WHEN TO GO

	JAN	FEB	MAR	APR	MAY	JUN	JUL	AUG	SEP	OCT	NOV	DEC
°C	17°C	17°C	19°C	23C	26°C	30°C	32°C	33°C	31°C	27°C	22°C	19°C
°F	63°F	63°F	66°F	73°F	79°F	86°F	90°F	91°F	88°F	81°F	72°F	66°F

High season Low season

Temperatures shown above are the average daily maximum for each month on the south coast; there are small variations on the north, west and east coasts. In Nicosia, temperatures are approximately an average of 5°C (9°F) higher in summer and 5°C (9°F) lower in the winter; the Troodos Mountains are an average 10°C (18°F) cooler than the rest of the country.

The best weather is between March and May and September and November since July and August are very hot and dry.

In winter there are some mild spells, mixed with heavy rain. Snow usually falls in December and January in the Troodos Mountains.

WHAT YOU NEED

		UK	Germany	USA	Canada	Australia	Ireland	Netherlands	Spain
● Required	Some countries require a passport to remain valid for a minimum period (usually at least six months) beyond the date of entry – check before you travel.								
○ Suggested									
▲ Not required									
Passport (or National Identity Card where applicable)		●	●	●	●	●	●	●	●
Visa (regulations can change – check before you travel)		▲	▲	▲	▲	▲	▲	▲	▲
Onward or Return Ticket		▲	▲	▲	▲	▲	▲	▲	▲
Health Inoculations (tetanus and polio)		▲	▲	▲	▲	▲	▲	▲	▲
Health Documentation (➤ 23, Health Insurance)		●	●	●	●	●	●	●	●
Travel Insurance		○	○	○	○	○	○	○	○
Driver's Licence (national)		●	●	●	●	●	●	●	●
Car Insurance Certificate		○	○	n/a	n/a	n/a	○	○	○
Car Registration Document		●	●	n/a	n/a	n/a	●	●	●

WEBSITES

Cyprus Tourist Organization
www.visitcyprus.com

North Cyprus Tourist Information
www.northcyprus.cc

TOURIST OFFICES AT HOME

In the UK

Cyprus Tourist Office
17 Hanover Street,
London W1S 1YP
☎ 020 7569 8800

North Cyprus Tourism Centre
29 Bedford Square,
London WC1B 3EG
☎ 020 7631 1930

In the USA

Cyprus Tourism Organization
13 East 40th Street
New York, NY 10016
☎ 212/683 5280

North Cyprus Tourism Centre
1667 K Street, Suite 690,
Washington DC 20006
☎ 202/887 6198

HEALTH INSURANCE

Tourists get free emergency medical treatment at government general
hospital accident and emergency departments; other services are paid for.
For UK nationals benefits are available in the Republic by arrangement
with the Department of Health before departure. Medical insurance is
advised for all.

Dental treatment must be paid for by all visitors. Hotels can generally
give recommendations for local dentists. Private medical insurance is
strongly advised for all tourists to cover costs of any dental treatment
in Cyprus.

TIME DIFFERENCES

GMT	Cyprus	Spain	USA (NY)	USA (West Coast)	Sydney
12 noon	2PM	1PM	7AM	4AM	10PM

Cyprus is on Eastern European Time from late March to late October
(GMT+2). From late October to late March the time is GMT+3.

NATIONAL HOLIDAYS

1 Jan *New Year's Day*
6 Jan *Epiphany*
25 Mar *Greek National Day*
1 Apr *Cyprus National Day*
Apr *Orthodox Easter*
1 May *Labour Day*

May/Jun *Pentecost/ Kataklysmos (Festival of the Flood)*
15 Aug *Assumption of Our Lady*
1 Oct *Cyprus Independence Day*

28 Oct *Greek National ('Ohi') Day*
24–26 Dec *Christmas*

Banks, businesses, museums and most shops are closed on these days.

WHAT'S ON WHEN

January *New Year's Day* (1 Jan)
Epiphany (6 Jan): important Greek Orthodox religious celebration.
March *Greek National Day* (25 Mar): parades and celebrations.
April *National Sovereignty and Turkish Children's Festival* (23 Apr).
May *Labour Day* (1 May).
May Fair in Pafos (1 May): 10 days of cultural events; exhibitions of flora, basketwork and embroidery.
Anthestiria Flower Festivals (early May): the festivals' origins go back to celebrations honouring the god Dionysos in ancient Greece.
Turkish Youth Festival (19 May).
Cyprus International Fair (late May): the largest trade fair in Cyprus, held in Nicosia and lasting 10 days.
June/July *International Famagusta Festival*: music, theatre, ballet, visual arts.
July *Belapais Music Festival*: Programme of chamber music, choral music and recitals.
Larnaka Festival (throughout Jul): dance and theatre in the fort and the Pattichon amphitheatre.
Peace and Freedom Day (20 Jul): date of Turkish intervention in 1974, public holiday in the North.
August *Turkish Communal Resistance Day* (1 Aug).
Turkish Victory Day (30 Aug).
August/September *Güzelyurt Orange Festival*: Folk music, concerts and dances.
Limassol Wine Festival (late Aug–first week in Sep): a 12-day festival, with music and dance.

Mehmetcik Grape Festival: celebrate with wine tastings, and there's a contest to select a Grape King and Queen.

October *Independence Day* (1 Oct).
Greek National Day (28 Oct): also known as Ohi Day. Parades in the South.
Turkish National Day (29 Oct).
November *Proclamation of Turkish Republic of North Cyprus* (15 Nov).
December *Christmas Day* (25 Dec).

Moveable feasts

Carnival/Apokreo Festivities (begins 2 weeks before Orthodox Lent): two weeks of fun. Limassol has fancy dress balls and children's parades.
Belapais International Music Festival (dates vary).
Green Monday (First day of Orthodox Lent): a day of laughter, funny disguises, feasting and vegetarian picnics in the country.
Procession of Agios Lazaros Icon, Larnaka (eight days before Orthodox Easter Sun): a special Mass service in memory of Agios Lazaros, followed by an impressive procession carrying his icon through the town.
Easter: the biggest Greek Orthodox religious feast – on the Sunday, celebrations last all day.
Kataklysmos, Festival of the Flood (50 days after Easter, coinciding with Pentecost): celebrations take place in all the seaside towns and include dancing, folk singing, swimming competitions and boat races.
Agia Napa Festival (Sep): a weekend of folk music, dance and theatre, combined with agricultural exhibitions.

Seker Bayrami or Ramazan Bayrami: a three-day feast at the end of the Ramadan fast.
Kurban Bayram: four days during which lambs are traditionally sacrificed and shared with the needy.

Getting there

BY AIR

Larnaka Airport

5km (3 miles) to city centre   🚗 10 minutes

Pafos Airport

                                    🚌 15 minutes

10km (6 miles) to city centre   🚗 15 minutes

Ercan Airport

15km (9 miles) to Nicosia city centre   🚌 15 minutes

REPUBLIC OF CYPRUS

South Cyprus has two main international airports, Larnaka and Pafos. Both are served by the national airline Cyprus Airways (tel: 2236 5700; www.cyprusairways.com). The two airports and Limassol Harbour are the only recognized points of entry for international visitors.

If you travel to the North and are not a citizen of the European Union, you may be refused entry to the South.

Larnaka Airport There is no bus service to and from the airport, but taxis are plentiful.

Pafos Airport Buses run six times a day between the city and airport. Taxis to Pafos are inexpensive, but onward fares rise sharply.

NORTH CYPRUS

International flights arrive at Ercan Airport. There is no public transport from the airport, but taxis run to Nicosia, Keryneia and Famagusta.

BY SEA

Ferries from Turkey arrive at Keryneia and Famagusta harbours.

Getting around

PUBLIC TRANSPORT
REGIONAL BUSES

Republic of Cyprus A number of intercity buses operate frequently between towns and various holiday resorts. Almost all villages are connected by local buses to nearest towns, but services operate only on weekdays, once a day, leaving in early morning and returning in the afternoon.

North Cyprus On the main routes such as Nicosia to Keryneia (Girne), Famagusta (Gazimağusa) or Morfou (Güzelyurt), buses operate frequently, departing when full.

BOAT TRIPS

Republic of Cyprus One-day boat excursions (usually including lunch) operate from April to October for visitors to the island. A choice of trips is on offer, including Limassol Harbour to Lady's Mile Beach; Pafos Harbour to Coral Bay and Agios Georgios; Larnaka Marina along Larnaka, Agia Napa and Protaras; Agia Napa to Paralimni and Protaras; and Lakki along the Akamas coast.

North Cyprus From May to October there are boat trips (including lunch) from Keryneia (Girne) Harbour to the beaches at Acapulco and Alagadi, or to Alsancak, Lapta and Karşiyaka.

URBAN TRANSPORT

Republic of Cyprus Urban and suburban buses operate frequently during the day between 5:30am and 7pm. During summer, in tourist areas, buses may operate until midnight. Check routes with your hotel.

North Cyprus There are good bus services within the main towns, with buses running frequently. Check with your hotel for routes.

TAXIS

In the Republic service taxis, shared with other people (4 to 7 seats), operate between main towns, departing when full. There are also rural taxis in hill resorts and urban taxis in towns.

In the North taxis can be found at taxi stands in most towns.

DRIVING

- Drive on the left.
- Speed limits on motorways and dual carriageways:
  100kph (62mph); min 65kph (40mph).
  Speed limits on country roads:
  80kph (50mph) (North Cyprus: 65kph/40mph).
  Speed limits on urban roads:
  50kph (31mph), or as signposted
- Seatbelts must be worn in front seats, and in rear seats where fitted.
- Random breath-testing takes place. Never drive under the influence of alcohol.
- Fuel in the north and the Republic of Cyprus is expensive, on a par with the rest of Europe. Grades sold are super, regular, unleaded and diesel. Fuel stations in the south open 6am–6pm, with automatic credit card/cash vending at other times. In the north they may open until 9 or 10pm.
- If you break down in the Republic of Cyprus a 24-hour towing service is provided by the Cyprus Automobile Association in Nicosia (tel: 2231 3233).
- If the car is rented follow the instructions given in your documentation.

CAR RENTAL

The many firms on the island include internationally known companies, though there are also local ones in the north and south. Cars, especially out of season, are moderately priced in the Republic and the North.

Drivers must usually be aged between 25 and 75 and have had a licence for more than a year. Some companies only accept international driver's licences; check if booking online.

FARES AND CONCESSIONS

Students Cyprus is not really on the backpacker route, but there are youth hostels in Nicosia, Larnaka, Pafos and in the Troodos Mountains. For details contact The Cyprus Youth Hostel Association, 34 Theodotv Street, Nicosia (tel: 2267 0027). The youth card 'Euro<26' secures discounts for ages 13–26 on a range of products. Contact the Youth Board of Cyprus, 62 Leoforos Aglantzias, Nicosia (tel: 2240 2600; www.youthboard.org.cy).

Senior citizens Few concessions are made to elderly visitors. Most hotels offer discounts during the low season but these are available to all age groups.

Being there

TOURIST OFFICES
Republic of Cyprus
- Cyprus Tourism Organization
  PO Box 24535
  CY 1390 Nicosia
  ☎ 2269 1100
  www.visitcyprus.com
- 11 Odos Aristokyprou
  Laiki Geitonia
  Nicosia
  ☎ 2269 1100
- 115A Odos Spyrou Araouzou
  Limassol
  ☎ 2536 2756
- Plateia Vasileos Pavlou
  Larnaka
  ☎ 2465 4322
- 3 Odos Gladstonos
  Pafos
  ☎ 2693 2841
- 12 Leoforos Kryou Nerou
  Agia Napa
  ☎ 2372 1796
- 2 Odos Vasileos Stasioikou Polis
  ☎ 2632 2468

Northern Cyprus
- Kyrenia Gate, Nicosia
  ☎ 227 2994
- Girne Harbour, Keryneia
  ☎ 815 2145
- Famagusta
  ☎ 366 2864

TIPS/GRATUITIES

	Yes ✓ No ✗	
Hotels (service included)	✓	5%
Restaurants (service included)	✓	5%
Cafés/bars (service included)	✓	round up
Taxis	✓	round up
Tour guides	✓	optional
Porters	✓	€1 per bag
Toilets	✗	

MONEY

The currency of the Republic is the euro (€), divided into 100 cents. Coins are in denominations of 1, 2, 5, 10, 20 and 50 cents and 1 and 2 euros; notes 5, 10, 20, 50, 100, 200, and 500 euros. The currency of the north is the New Turkish Lira (YTL), although UK pounds, euros and US dollars are widely accepted. Exchange travellers' cheques at banks, bureaux de change and hotels. Most banks have ATMs. Most currencies are accepted at banks and exchanges in both zones.

POSTAL AND INTERNET SERVICES

There are main post offices in the main towns.
Republic: open Mon–Fri 7:30–1:30 (Thu also 3–6).
North: open Mon–Fri 8–1, 2–5, Sat 8:30–12:30.
Internet services: Internet cafés are everywhere, and most hotels in the South offer WiFi or have a computer for guest use.

TELEPHONES

Public telephones are found in town centres. In the South they take coins or *telecards* (available from kiosks). Payphones in the North only accept phone cards.

Emergency telephone numbers

Police assistance:
☎ 112 (Republic)
☎ 155 (North)

Fire:
☎ 112 (Republic)
☎ 199 (North)

Ambulance:
☎ 112 (Republic and North)

International dialling codes

From Cyprus to
UK: 00 44
USA: 00 1

Netherlands: 00 31
Spain: 00 34
Germany: 00 49

Directory Enquiries

Local:
☎ 11892 (Republic)
☎ 192 (North)

International:
☎ 11894 (Republic)
☎ 192 (North)

EMBASSIES AND CONSULATES

UK
☎ 2286 1100 (Republic)
☎ 228 3861 (North)

Germany
☎ 2245 1145 (Republic)
☎ 227 5161 (North)

USA
☎ 2239 3939 (Republic)
☎ 227 8295 (North)

Netherlands
☎ 2287 3666 (Republic)

Spain
☎ 2245 014 0 (Republic)

HEALTH ADVICE

Sun advice Cyprus enjoys almost constant sunshine for most of the year. Wear a hat and drink plenty of fluids during the hot months (particularly July and August). A high-protection sunscreen is also recommended.

Drugs Minor ailments can be dealt with at pharmacies *(farmakio* in the south, *eczane* in the north). Some drugs available only on prescription elsewhere are available over the counter.

Safe water Tap water in hotels, restaurants and public places is generally safe to drink though not always very palatable. Bottled water is widely available and inexpensive.

PERSONAL SAFETY

The police are relaxed and helpful and English is often spoken. In tourist areas in the south, Cyprus Tourism

Organization representatives can provide a degree of assistance. However, crime in Cyprus is at a reassuringly low level. Take the usual precautions with regard to handbags and valuables left in cars and lock them away, out of sight. Any thefts or offences should be reported to the police, if only for insurance purposes.

● Do not try to cross the Green Line (the dividing line between the two parts) except at official crossing points.

● Do not enter military zones (north or south).

● Do not use roads marked as blocked-off on a map (they may encroach on military zones).

ELECTRICITY
The power supply is 240 volts.

Type of socket: Square, taking three-square-pin plugs (as UK), and round two-pin sockets taking two-round-pin (continental-style) plugs.

SUMMER OPENING HOURS (REPUBLIC)

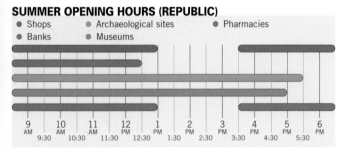

SUMMER OPENING HOURS (NORTH)

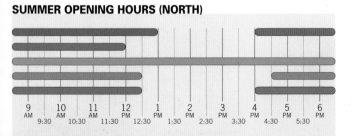

LANGUAGE

Cyprus has two official languages, Greek and Turkish. Greek is spoken in the Republic of Cyprus and Turkish in the north. Most Greek Cypriots speak English but an attempt at the language is useful, for example in a village coffee shop and similar places where locals may not know English. In the north things are different – not as much English is spoken. Waiters and others have only a limited vocabulary and some knowledge of Turkish is an advantage. Below are some words that you may come across.

ENGLISH	GREEK	TURKISH
yes	ne	evet
no	óhi	hayir
please	parakaló	lütfen
thank you	efcharistó	tesekkür ederim
hello	yásas, yásoo	merhaba
goodbye	yásas, yásoo	hosça kal
sorry	signómi	özür dilerim
how much?	póso?	ne kadar?
I (don't) understand	(dhen) katalavéno	sizi anliyorum
hotel	xenodhohío	otel
room	dhomátyo	oda
… single/double	monó/dhipló	tek/iki kishilik
breakfast	proinó	kahvalti
toilet	twaléta	tuvalet
bath	bányo	banyo
shower	doos	dus
balcony	balkóni	balkon
restaurant	estiatório	restoran
café	kafenío	bar
menu	menóo	menü
lunch	yévma	ögle yemegi
dinner	dhípno	aksam yemegi
dessert	epidhórpyo	tatli
waiter	garsóni	garson
the bill	loghariazmós	hesap

Best places to see

1 Agios Ilarion

This fortified former monastery, besieged and taken by Richard the Lionheart in 1191, has spectacular coastal views.

Richard the Lionheart laid siege to the castle, and after four days the Byzantine ruler Isaac Comnenos surrendered. Today the Turkish military controls the heights around the castle, and it is a significant place to advertise their presence.

This is no compact, easily visited site. There are lower, middle and upper wards, with quite a distance between each and a steep climb to the upper section. The big compensation for the effort – fairly substantial in the summer heat – is the unbelievable view. The north shore is directly below and mainland Turkey is plainly visible in the clear air of the cooler months. East and west a spectacular line of peaks and ridges runs into the distance.

St Hilarion, it seems, was a recluse who found refuge on these heights, and built a retreat here. A monastery was established on the site in the 11th century, and was later fortified and then extended by the Lusignans. The lower ward housed the garrison and their horses. A tunnel leads on to the middle ward and a small Byzantine church. Some steps descend to a hall,

which may have been a refectory or banqueting chamber. Adjacent is a belvedere and café. The view over the coast is exceptional.

The path to the upper ward climbs steadily to the mountain top. Even then not everything is accessible, although St John's Tower, in its precipitous location, can be reached by a short detour. The Queen's Window is perhaps the ideal place to stop and rest.

✚ 16K ✉ High in the hills west of Keryneia (Girne)
🕐 Jun–Sep daily 9–4; Oct–May daily 9–6 ✋ Moderate
🍴 Café at the gate (€)

2 Akamas Peninsula

A beautiful region of hills, valleys and rocky shores, ideal for rambling, with rich and varied flora and diverse wildlife.

This westernmost extremity is unique in the Greek Cypriot south of the island, not only for its beauty but also for the absence of tourist development. Three areas are now designated as protected national parks and no development is permitted although hunting still occurs in winter.

The vegetation is Mediterranean, with large tracts of impenetrable *maquis* interspersed with a thin covering of pine trees, olive trees and juniper. Autumn flowering cyclamen is everywhere. In places the landscape is impressively stark, with spectacular rock outcrops. On the beaches green and loggerhead turtles still come up to lay their eggs, and occasionally a monk seal may be sighted. Although there are no metalled roads

after the tourist pavilion, the area is becoming popular with trailbikers and walkers.

Several trails for ramblers have been created, starting at the Baths of Aphrodite, west of Polis. A network of marked paths traverses the hills and information panels outline the types of flora. These are described in a free booklet from the tourist office called *Nature Trails of the Akamas*. The ascent of Mouti tis Sotiras is worth contemplating: it only takes an hour to reach the summit and the view is superb. Needless to say, in summer it is a hot and sticky expedition. An alternative is to take a boat from Lakki for a swim and a picnic in one of the delightful coves, perhaps near Fontana Amoroza (Love's Spring), halfway to Cape Arnaoutis.

✚ 1E ✉ The westernmost peninsula 🍴 Baths of Aphrodite Tourist Pavilion Café (€€) 🛈 Across the road from the café, and at the end of a short path and under trees is the pool called the Baths of Aphrodite

3 Hala Sultan Tekke and Salt Lake

A Muslim holy shrine standing on the shore of a natural landmark, which has very different aspects in winter and summer.

For Turkish Cypriots, the Hala Sultan Tekke's importance is surpassed only by the shrines of Mecca, Medina and al Aksa (Jerusalem). It was here that the prophet Mohammed's maternal aunt, Umm Haram, was buried in AD649. Apparently, she fell from a donkey and broke her neck while participating in an Arab raid on the island. Three enormous stones were raised to mark her grave and the site became an important place of pilgrimage for Muslims.

The mosque, with its distinctive dome and minaret, was built by the Turks in 1816, though the tomb dates from 1760. Visitors can enter the mosque but must respect the dress code and remove their shoes before entering; women should also cover their heads with a scarf.

In the summer the surrounding gardens are a relatively cool haven from the heat of the Salt Lake. This is dry for much of the year, but in winter the lake fills with water and attracts a wide range of migrating birds. The most spectacular of the winter visitors are the flamingos, whose distinctive

pink colour makes an attractive sight, though their numbers have greatly reduced in recent years. In summer the water evaporates, leaving a dusty grey expanse that shimmers in the heat.

The salt was once a significant product in the island's economy, but today it is no longer economically viable to collect. It originates from the nearby sea, seeping up through the porous rocks during the rainy months.

✚ 11C ✉ 3km (2 miles) west of Larnaka on the Kiti road 🕐 Apr–Oct daily 8–7; Nov–Mar daily 8–5 💰 Free, but donation requested 🍴 Taverna (€€) 🚌 Bus from Larnaka with drop-off on the main road

4 Kourion

Kourion is the most important archaeological site in the Greek Cypriot south, impressively perched on the cliffs overlooking the sea.

There has been a settlement here since 3300BC, but the earliest remains date back to the late Classical and mainly Hellenistic periods (325–50BC) while most of the visible structures belong to the imperial Roman period (50BC–AD395). It went into decline as it suffered from Arab raiders and the population moved inland. Excavations started in 1873 and have continued ever since.

The Theatre presents the most striking image of the whole site. It seated an audience of 3,500 and was probably built by the early Greeks and then extended by the Romans to allow for gladiatorial combat and for man against animal spectacles.

The Annexe of Eustolios lies just uphill from the Theatre and has an impressive mosaic floor. Further up the hill are the Baths, which also had mosaic floors. The Baths follow the Roman pattern, with a *frigidarium* (cold room), then a *tepidarium* (warm room) and a *caldarium* (hot baths). Mechanisms for heating the water, along with furnaces and tanks, are in evidence.

At the top of the hill west of the Theatre is the Building of the Achilles Mosaic. Constructed around a courtyard, it has a mosaic showing Achilles in disguise revealing his true identity to Odysseus by mistake. There is also a depiction of Ganymede and the Eagle. The house dates from about AD4. A similar house a short

distance down the track has a mosaic showing two gladiators in combat. Also visible are the remains of an aqueduct that brought the settlement's water supply to the Fountain House, traces of which can still be seen. Opposite the Fountain House is the Basilica, which was built in the 5th century. It has fragments of mosaics on the floor and the roof was once supported by 12 columns.

This site covers the main areas of interest, but about 1km (0.5 miles) towards Pafos is the openly accessible Stadium, which once seated 6,000.

✠ 6B ✉ Off the Limassol–Pafos road ☎ 2593 4250
🕑 Apr–May, Sep–Oct daily 8–6; Jun–Aug daily 8–7:30;
Nov–Mar daily 8–5. Excavations on the site can close some parts at times 🎫 Inexpensive 🍴 Kiosk in the nearby tourist pavilion (€, closed in winter) 🚌 From Limassol ❓ Classical plays or productions of Shakespeare are performed through summer. The tourist office will have the programme

5 Lara

Lara is the name of a headland on the west coast with sandy bays on each side. This splendid stretch of coast continues up to Koppos Island, opposite which the rough road peters out, and then on to the distant northern cape.

The nearest outpost is Agios Georgios, a town with a church and excellent seafood restaurants. It sees the last of the bitumen road, and from now on the track is a well-graded dirt and gravel road, although after rain it gets muddy in parts. And there is quite a lot of it – 8km (5 miles) in all, with one steep area. Thicket, thorn and mimosa border the road, and only by chance or local knowledge can sandy coves on the rocky shore be found. The beaches of Lara itself are easier to discover, with a sweeping bay to the north and a smaller one to the south.

Lara is now a popular excursion destination and there are regular boat trips from Pafos, calling at Agios Georgios on the way. Such splendid beaches

and scenery would attract visitors in any circumstances, but there is a further incentive – Lara's famous sea turtles. In an attempt to secure the future of these beleaguered and precious amphibians, a hatchery has been established at Lara. Its opening was accompanied by great publicity and many make the trip in the hope of seeing them; in fact there is no certainty of this – much depends on the cycle of the breeding season. The future of this beautiful and ecologically important coastline has been secured since the government declared that no building development was permitted in the area.

✚ 1D ✉ Western Cyprus, north of Pafos 🍴 Tavernas on the headland of Agios Georgios, of which Saint George is the best (€)

Nicosia Walled City

www.nicosia.org.cy

Eleven stout bastions, an enormous moat and a massive circular wall give the city its distinctive and unique plan. Much has survived across the centuries.

Nicosia's formidable walls, so masterfully constructed by the Venetians, remain substantially intact, though Pafos Gate to the west is battered and Girne (Keryneia) Gate's situation ruined. Famagusta Gate has fared better, although the cultural centre housed within it, perhaps something of a comedown for what was the important eastern entrance into the city, is currently closed. A lesser

indignity has been inflicted on the moat (always intended to be dry): this deep and formidable barrier to full-scale attack is now gardens, car parks and football pitches. In the end the great walls did not save Nicosia. The Turks broke through in 1570 after a bloody siege that lasted 70 days.

Today Lidras and Onasagoras streets, in the Greek Cypriot sector, are thriving places, and small shops are always busy. A little to the east the reconstructed buildings in the Laiki Geitonia quarter (➤ 147) are popular. In the Turkish Cypriot part development moves at a somewhat slower pace.

Along the back streets some areas are conspicuously decrepit. This is not always to be regretted, as low overheads have enabled a Bohemian quarter to develop off Anasagorou Street, with bars, cafés and an arts centre. Close by, and including Odos Ermou, is a renovated neighbourhood. The buildings, mainly houses, remain much as before, but have been refurbished. Small interesting squares, once rough underfoot, are now smoothly paved.

Of course, Nicosia is the city of the Green Line, a barrier of sandbags and barbed wire that can now be crossed at the Ledra Palace Crossing, erected before the conscripts who now guard it were born.

🚩 16K ✉ Centre of Nicosia 🍴 Cafés at Laiki Geitonia, Famagusta Gate, Atatürk Meydanı (€)

7 Pafos Archaeological Park

Roman houses with impressive and well-preserved mosaics depicting colourful scenes from Greek mythology.

The mosaics were discovered in five large 3rd century AD villas that probably belonged to wealthy Roman noblemen (one was presumably the governor's palace). The House of Dionysos was excavated first, after a passing shepherd turned up some fragments of mosaics. The depictions include Ganymede being taken to Olympus by an eagle.

The most famous mosaic illustrates the triumph of Dionysos as he heads across the skies in a chariot drawn by leopards. According to the legend, Dionysos was the first person to discover how to make wine, and his followers are depicted enjoying the fruits of his labour.

The House of Aion displays a fine series of late 4th-century mosaics, which were discovered in 1983. The five scenes starting from the top left show Leda and the Swan; the baby Dionysos; then the middle panel portrays a beauty contest being judged by Aion; on the bottom row is the triumphant procession of Dionysos and the punishment of a musician, Marsyas, who had challenged Apollo to a musical contest and lost.

The House of Orpheus contains representations of Amazons, Hercules and the Lion of Nemea, alongside an impressive mosaic of Orpheus.

The main mosaic in the House of Theseus is that of Theseus killing the minotaur, although there are some others too. The mosaics here are less well preserved than in other areas. A newer discovery – the House of the Four Seasons – was unearthed in 1992. Mosaics showing the Gods of the Seasons and a variety of hunting scenes were found here. As excavations are continuing, parts of these houses may not be open to the public.

Also within the park are a Roman theatre, the Odeion (➤ 124) and the a 7th-century fort, the Saranta Kolones (➤ 127).

🚩 *Pafos 1b* ✉ A short distance inland from the harbour
☎ 2630 6217 🕐 Jun–Aug daily 8–7:30; Sep–May daily 8–5. Closed 1 Jan, 25 Dec, Greek Orthodox Easter Sun
✋ Moderate (includes Odeion and Saranta Kolones)
🍴 Cafés at the harbour (€€)

8 Panagia tou Kikkou

The monastery is the largest and richest religious foundation in Cyprus and is known throughout the Orthodox world for its many walls, courtyards and colonnades decorated with magnificent gold mosaics.

Kykkou is high and alone in the hills of western Cyprus, but even at 1,318m (4,324ft) above sea level it is overlooked by higher ground. In summer its cloisters and courtyards are cool; in winter, when the mist descends, the temperature drops

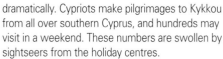

dramatically. Cypriots make pilgrimages to Kykkou from all over southern Cyprus, and hundreds may visit in a weekend. These numbers are swollen by sightseers from the holiday centres.

Kykkou was built about 900 years ago to house its icon, the painting of which is attributed to St Luke and was given to a Cypriot monk by Byzantine Emperor Alexius Comnenos for relieving his daughter's sciatica. The present construction is not of great antiquity – fires destroyed earlier buildings and nothing remains from before the 19th century.

In contrast with the spartan conditions of earlier times, today's monks have many modern comforts. Even so, the community has dwindled from hundreds to a handful, and even fewer novices.

There is also a small museum with items of interest from the monastery's past, mainly religious regalia and books. The famous icon is called Eleousa. It has been encased in silver for 200 years and anyone attempting to gaze directly on it does so under sufferance of horrible punishment. Photography is not permitted within the museum.

In 1926 a novice called Michaïl Mouskos came to the monastery. He later became Archbishop Makarios III, and president of Cyprus. During the 1950s EOKA campaign the monastery was used by the guerillas for communications and the handling of supplies. Makarios is buried on the hill called Throni, directly above the monastery.

🚌 4D ✉ West of Pedoulas, western Troodos ☎ Museum: 2294 2736 ⏱ Monastery: daily early morning to dusk. Museum: Jun–Oct daily 10–6; Nov–May daily 10–4 💶 Free; museum expensive 🍴 Cafés nearby (€)

Salamis

In legend the founder of Salamis, an impressive archaeological site, was the Greek hero Teucer, brother of Ajax and son of Telamon.

In the 11th century BC Salamis was the first city of Cyprus. It was not until the Roman occupation centuries later that it was succeeded by Pafos in the west. There was much rebuilding due to earthquakes: in AD350 the Byzantines changed the city's name to Constantia and restored it as the capital, but in the 7th century Arab attacks left the city in ruins.

In high summer a visit is a memorable occasion, although only the most determined will be able to stay the full course in the great heat. However, the Roman Theatre should not be missed, with its restored tiers of seats rising to an impressive height.

A little further north are the vents and hypocausts of the Baths, opening on to the Gymnasium, all built by the Romans. This structure, its rows of marble columns plainly evident, was damaged by earthquakes and remodelled in Byzantine times, only to collapse later. The columns that we see today were re-erected in the 1950s.

South of the Theatre the huge columns of the granite Forum lie across the site. To the east are the few remains of the church of Agios Epifanios, built in the 4th century. This northern section of the site was a cultural centre. The Agora is found in the

central part, near the Voutra, a cistern that functioned until the 7th century. Close by are the ruins of the Temple of Zeus.

Walk some 500m (550yds) northeast, towards the sea, and you will come to the Kampanopetra, a large Early Christian basilica, which has been only partially excavated. The Ancient Harbour is about 300m (330yds) southeast, on the shoreline. Alternatively, cross the main road and walk about 200m (220yds) to the western site. Here, at the Royal Necropolis, are several important tombs. These were designed for rich citizens, though there are also tombs for ordinary people nearby, called the Cellarka.

✚ 21J ✉ 10km (6 miles) north of Famagusta (Gazimağusa)
⚅ Apr–Oct daily 9–7; Nov–Mar daily 9–5 🎫 Expensive
🍴 Café near north entrance (€)

10 Troodos Mountains

Despite their elevation, the Troodos Mountains are mostly rounded hills with a multitude of charming villages hidden in the pine-clad folds.

The Troodos is an extensive area, running from west of Larnaka to the high ground of Mount Olympos, then falling gradually to the western coast. There are many reasons for taking in the delights of the mountains, and they make a refreshing change from the hot beaches and dusty lowlands. Terraced vineyards shape the lower southern slopes, with Aleppo pine covering the higher ground. Summits may be tree covered or adorned with spiky scrub, relieved occasionally with dried flowers. Northern slopes are different again: dark poplars stand out in the valleys alongside golden oak and rock rose. Summer days are cooler on the high ground and a big attraction in winter is the snow, with skiing on Mount Olympos.

The most impressive of Cyprus's celebrated monasteries are in the Troodos. Chrysorrogiatissa

(➤ 132–133), standing in splendid terrain, is about 45km (28 miles) from Pafos. Kykkou (➤ 50–51) is more convenient for Limassol, but still half a day's excursion. In the east is Machairas (➤ 153–154), less splendid, but well worth a visit.

Regrettably few seek out the small Byzantine churches of Panagia tou Araka (➤ 155) and Stavros tou Agiasmati near Lagoudera on the north side of the range. This is understandable because it is a long drive, but their frescoes are extraordinary.

Walks and trails are now popular in Cyprus, and those above Platres (Kalidonia Falls and around Mount Olympos) are detailed in a booklet produced by the tourist office. In western Cyprus the forest takes over, and Cedar Valley (➤ 78) is renowned for its giant cedars. Fortunately for the peace of this marvellous area few people seem prepared to negotiate the difficult roads.

✚ 4D ✉ Central Cyprus 🍴 Cafés at Troodos resort, Platres, Foini, Kakopetria and other villages (€–€€)

Best things to do

Great places to have lunch

Bunch of Grapes Inn
The old building is full of charm and the menu a blend of traditional Cypriot dishes and international cuisine.
✉ Pissouri village ☎ 2522 1275

Faros Fish Tavern
Simple, fresh seafood served overlooking the sea. Popular with locals and visitors alike.
✉ Governor's Beach ☎ 2563 2552

Melanda Beach Restaurant
Specializes in seafood. Situated at the edge of the unspoiled beach.
✉ Avdimou Beach (not the jetty), 30km (18.5 miles) west of Limassol
☎ 0956 5336

Petra tou Romiou Restaurant
Fabulous views over the famous Rock of Aphrodite.
✉ Petra tou Romiou ☎ 2699 9005

Saint George
Serving up the freshest seafood on the west coast, this is
the place to head for superb fried fish and chips.
✉ Agios Georgiou, near Pafos ☎ 2662 1306

Trypiti
With its excellent seafood this newcomer is providing
some stiff competition to the 'Harbour' monopoly.
✉ Keryneia harbour ☎ 838 7070

Vangelis
For something traditional try the pigeon or rabbit. Popular
with locals.
✉ Paralimni on the Deryneia road ☎ 2382 1456

Vassos
Famed for its fresh seafood, generous portions and
waterfront location, Vassos is the local favourite.
✉ Agia Napa harbour ☎ 2372 1884

Yiangos and Peter Taverna
Fine harbour view; seafood straight off the fishing boats.
✉ Harbour, Latsi ☎ 2632 1411

Handicrafts

Basketry Hand-woven reed baskets are made at Liopetri, Xylofagou and Sotira, near Agia Napa, and at Geroskipou.

Ceramics Craft pottery centres include Geroskipou, Koloni, Kornos and Foini. In the north, visit the Ceramic Centre at Ortakioi (Ortaköy; ➤ 185).

Embroidery Hand-embroidered *lefkaritika* lace is made at Lefkara (➤ 112, 119). Fine lace is also made in North Cyprus.

Glassware Omodos has several glass workshops.

Gourds These are made into plant pots and vases.

Honey Widely available; some convents harvest excellent honey.

Icons Made at Agia Varnava Monastery and Panagia Chrysorrogiatissa (➤ 132–133).

Leather Leather bags, belts and jackets are widely available.

Silver Lefkara is noted for its silverware (➤ 112, 119), as is northern Cyprus.

Weaving Handloom-woven striped, brightly coloured *lefkonika* cloth is made at Fyti (➤ 139).

Woodwork Items are usually made from olive-tree wood and you will see workshops as you drive around the countryside.

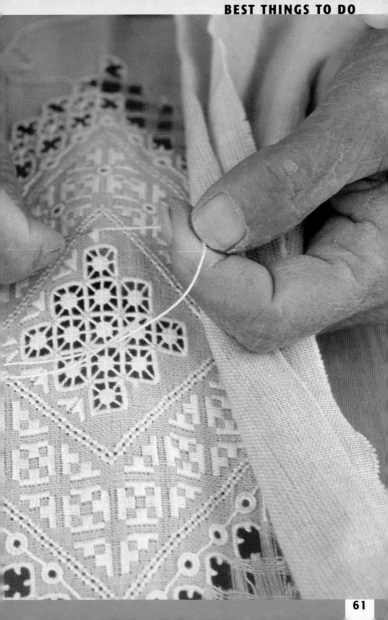

Archaeological Sites

Agios Ilarion (➤ 36–37)
This was a fortified monastery
whose ruins are in the
Pentadaktylos (Beşparmak)
Mountains.

Amathous (➤ 104)
These ruins in Limassol are
spread widely, and possibly
extend into the sea.

Choirokoitia (➤ 110)
This was home to a large
community in the 7th
century BC.

Kition (➤ 88)
The site of the remains of an
ancient city.

Kourion (➤ 42–43)
This is the south's most
important archaeological site.

Odeion (➤ 124)
These Roman ruins in Pafos
have been partially restored.

Pafos (▶ 48–49)
The city has a wealth of Roman remains, including some stunning mosaics.

Palaia Pafos (▶ 130–131) The ruins outide Pafos includes the Sanctuary of Aphrodite.

St Paul's Pillar (▶ 125)
The site is still undergoing excavation.

Salamis (▶ 52–53)
The leading city of Cyprus in the 11th century BC is a large and impressive site.

Sanctuary of Apollo Ylatis (▶ 114)
The temple was a place of worship for many centuries.

Tombs of the Kings (▶ 127)
Probably the tombs of noble families rather than royalty.

Activities

Cycling There are scores of bicycles for rent in all the resorts. Main roads can be very busy at weekends and the tourist office advises cyclists to avoid them at this time.

Diving Explorations of the wonders of the deep are well catered for at diving centres and some hotels around the island.

Golf One has to admire the Cypriots – nothing is too daunting to the designers of the island's golf courses: in rocky, arid landscapes they have created greens. This entrepreneurial boldness appears to have paid off with many 18-hole courses now well established (► 140).

Hill walks In summer it is very hot for walking. Nevertheless, interesting trails have been laid out in the Akamas and Troodos.

Horseback riding There are centres in Nicosia, Limassol and Pafos. Riding trails include countryside areas such as the Troodos Mountains.

Luxuriating spa treatments Increasingly popular, there is a wide range of spa treatements available at many hotels around the island.

Paragliding Incredibly, people queue for this expensive death-defying adventure. One nervous, critical leap and it is up into the thermals.

WATER SPORTS
Exciting There are more ways of following a motor boat than standing upright on two planks of wood. A multitude of flexible inflatables, including the notorious banana, skim the waves during high-speed tows. Some aficionados of the foam prefer the adrenalin boost of jet skis. Windsurfing and surfing are all popular

although some areas are unsuitable for these pursuits. Sailing is catered for, and there are also organized boat trips.

Sedate Relaxing pastimes include airbed floating and the ever-popular pedalos.

Swimming Few can resist the warm turquoise sea. You'll see every swimming technique known to man, and some others, performed with great virtuosity.

Places to take the children

Aphrodite Waterpark
Pools, splashes, spiral descents and more.
✉ Geroskipou, off Leoforos Poseidonos ☎ 2691 3638/2622 2722
🕐 Apr–Oct daily 10–6

Camel Park
Learn about camels and enjoy a ride, or take a swim in the pool.
✉ Mazotos, 20km (12 miles) southwest of Larnaka ☎ 2499 4243/9941 6968;
www.camel-park.com 🕐 Daily 9–7

Donkey Sanctuary
Unwanted donkeys end up here, cared for by two expatriates from
the UK. A visitor centre has information and refreshments.
✉ Vouni, 36km (22 miles) northwest of Limassol ☎ 2594 5488
🕐 Daily 10–4

Ocean Aquarium

Hundreds of species from the seas, plus landscaped grounds.

✉ 19 Leoforos Kavo Gkreko, Protaras, 5km (3 miles) north of the centre
☎ 2374 1111 🕓 Daily 10–6

Ostrich Wonderland Theme Park

Kids can learn about ostriches as they pet these curious creatures
at one of Europe's largest ostrich parks.

✉ Agios Ioannis Malountas ☎ 2299 1008 🕓 Daily 9–5

Pafos Bird Park

Parrots, hornbills, toucans, eagles and many more species.
Gazelles, giant tortoises and other reptiles plus an aquarium,
cinema and restaurant.

✉ Pegeia, on road north out of Coral Bay ☎ 2656 3947;
www.pafosbirdpark.com 🕓 Daily 9–sunset

Skiing on Mount Olympos

Kids can learn to ski with excellent instructors certified by the
Cyprus Ski Federation on the gentle beginner's slopes.

✉ Mount Olympos, Troodos Mountains ☎ www.cyprusski.com 🕓 Winter –
check snow conditions

Snake George's Reptile Park

George tries to improve public understanding of snakes at his
reptile park.

✉ 15km (9 miles) north of Pafos on coast road to Agios Georgios, behind EKO
petrol station ☎ 9998 7685 🕓 Daily 10–sunset

Wet 'n' Wild Waterpark

Chutes and other ingenious designs flush willing participants
through a multitude of coloured tubes.

✉ Off Limassol–Nicosia Highway, Mouttagiaka junction, Limassol
☎ 2531 8000 🕓 Apr–Oct daily 10–6

Great beaches

Avdimou Beach
Avdimou Beach (▶ 109) is a good long sandy stretch, though the water becomes deep very quickly. There is a small taverna and it is usually quiet, but at weekends it can be busy with service personnel and their families.

✉ 3km (2 miles) off main road, take turn-off signposted for the taverna

🍴 Taverna on beach (€)

Coral Bay
The small bay comes complete with hotels, shops and restaurants. The sea is a beautiful turquoise but the shoreline is being lost to development. The popular beach has sunbeds everywhere and water sports.

✉ 13km (8 miles) north of Pafos 🚌 10, 15 from Pafos lower town

🍴 Cafés on the clifftops (€€)

Famagusta Beach
Beautiful and sandy, near the ruined resort of Varosha.

Governor's Beach
The beach is backed by low white cliffs. The dark grey sand is its most distinctive feature and can get painfully hot by the middle of a summer's day. The beach, although narrow, is popular with local people and can be very busy on summer weekends.

✉ Junction 16 Nicosia–Limassol motorway

Karpasia (▶ 79).
This beautiful remote peninsula in North Cyprus has long stretches of pristine, sandy beaches, arguably the country's best.

Konnos Bay
North of Cape Gkreko (Greco), this bay has white sands and clear blue sea.

Lara
See pages 44–45.

Nissi Beach
Two kilometres (1 mile) outside Agia Napa. Very popular, this
beach gets jam-packed in summer (▶ 92).

Pissouri Bay
One of the few beaches in the area, it can get very busy
at times.

Pomos coast
This beautiful coast is noted for its quiet beaches (▶ 134).

Timi Beach
Sandy coves and waters that are quiet until the weekends.

Best museums

Byzantine Museum, Nicosia (➤ 144)
Within the Archbishop Makarios Cultural Centre this impressive museum displays some of the island's most important Byzantine icons and mosaics.

Cyprus Museum, Nicosia (➤ 144)
Home to the most important archaeological finds from across the island, from Kourion to Salamis, a visit here is a must before touring Cyprus's many ancient sites.

Geroskipou Folk Art Museum (➤ 130)
Set in a traditional stone house, this sprawling museum has a fascinating collection of traditional looms, domestic and farming implements, textiles, pottery, and costumes.

House of Hadjigeorgakis Kornesios (➤ 145)
Also known as the Grand Dragoman's House, this splendidly restored building is now an ethnographical museum housing the personal possessions and artefacts from the Haji's life.

Keryneia Castle (➤ 175)
Within the sprawling castle is the small but fascinating shipwreck museum, housing the blackened hull of a 2,300-year-old Hellenic-era merchant ship.

Kouklia Local Museum at Palaia Pafos (➤ 130–131)
A marble sarcophogus depicting images from Homer's epics,

lustrous pottery, painted jugs and pretty figurines are the highlights here.

Limassol District Archaeological Museum (➤ 107)
Cyprus's next most important collection of archaeological finds is on display at this fine little museum with a lovely garden.

Mevlevi Tekke Ethnographical Museum (➤ 150)
Once home to the intriguing Whirling Dervishes, an Islamic sect who spin themselves into euphoria, this small museum now houses a kitsch collection of Dervish mannequins, musical instruments and costumes.

Pierides Foundation Museum (➤ 89)
This elegant colonial house is home to the superb private collection of the wealthy Pierides family; there are more than 3,000 pieces, including important archaeological finds and traditional folk crafts.

a walk in Limassol (Lemesos)

The walk starts on the seafront by the car parks and sculpture park. Follow the promenade southwest to reach a small roundabout which marks the old harbour, complete with fishing boats. There is a small reptile house on one corner with local and foreign species.

Proceed inland to the 14th-century castle and Cyprus Medieval Museum (➤ 106–107). Turn right along Odos Genthliou Mitella and pass the Al-Kebir mosque, which is still in use.

This was once the Turkish part of the town and many of the older houses are of a typical Turkish design. The municipal fruit and vegetable market lies just east of the mosque.

Continue generally northeast until the road leads into Odos Agiou Andreou, the main shopping street.

There are many narrow alleyways in this area and they are interesting to explore, though walkers should not worry about getting lost as they will eventually emerge on to the wider thoroughfare. Odos Agiou Andreou has a wide selection of shops, with goods ranging from the usual souvenirs to leather goods and jewellery.

After about 1km (0.5 miles) Agia Trias Church can be visited a short way up Odos Agias Trias, just before Odos Zinonos Kitieos. Returning to the main road the Folk Art Museum is a little way on the left. One kilometre (0.5 miles) further along Odos Agiou Andreou, at the north side of the Municipal Gardens, turn right on Odos Kanningkos to reach the District Archaeological Museum (▶ 107), 200m (220yds) to the left. The walk ends in the Municipal Gardens, which offer peace after the busy city streets.

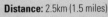

Distance: 2.5km (1.5 miles)
Time: 1–3.5 hours
Start point Seafront car park ✚ *Limassol 3b*
End point Municipal Gardens ✚ *Limassol 4c*
Lunch Many cafés around the castle (€) ✉ Odos Eirinis or La Mer (▶ 117, €)

Best views

Belapais Abbey
From its setting in the mountains, you see citrus and almond groves below and the sea in the distance (➤ 172).

Cape Gkreko (Greco)
The cape is fenced off, but there are views across the coastline from nearby cliffs.

Cape Kormakitis
On a clear day you can see the Taurus Mountains in Turkey from here.

Panagia Chrysorrogiatissa Monastery (➤ 132–133).
Views across the foothills of the Troodos Mountains.

Mount Olympos
Tremendous views across Cyprus (➤ 154–155).

Pomos Point
Stretch of coastline that has superb views (➤ 79).

Agios Ilarion Castle
Excellent views reward a stiff climb to the castle remains (➤ 36–37).

Stavrovouni
The monastery (➤ 95) has wonderful views across the Larnaka area and the coast.

Throni Hill
Views from the hill near Archbishop Makarios's tomb.

Tombs of the Kings
Sweeping views across the sea (➤ 127).

Places to stay

Anassa (€€€)

A palatial hotel with wonderful views of the Akamas Peninsula and sea, its landscaped gardens and generously sized rooms lend it an air of relaxed sophistication. Fine restaurants and an excellent spa.

✉ Polis Beach, Polis, Pafos region ☎ 2688 8000; www.thanoshotels.com

Bellapais Gardens (€€)

Perched on the slopes of Belapais, within walking distance of the famous monastery, this charming hotel ticks the boxes of personable service, privacy, pretty views and swimming pool. Good restaurant with breathtaking views.

✉ Crusader Road, Belapais ☎ 815 6066; www.bellapaisgardens.com

Columbia Beach Resort (€€€)

A fine resort on lovely Pissouri Bay, this has oodles of Mediterranean charm, enormous comfortable rooms, an inviting swimming pool, an outstanding spa and notable restaurants.

✉ Pissouri Bay ☎ 2583 3000; www.columbia-hotels.com

The Four Seasons (€€€)

No relation to the Four Seasons chain, this hotel does a remarkable job of offering the same level of service and amenities as the luxury brand. Expect welcoming public spaces and some of the best restaurants on the island under the one roof.

✉ Leoforos Amathous, Agios Tychonas ☎ 2585 8000; www.fourseasons.com.cy

Hilton Cyprus (€€€)

Nicosia's most expensive hotel, a prestigious establishment on elevated ground on the south side of the city, complete with large swimming pool and extensive facilities.

✉ Leoforos Archiepiskopou Makariou III, Nicosia ☎ 2237 7777; www.hilton.com

Karpaz Arch Houses (€€)

Set in a splendid, renovated stone building with a rather grand arch, these rooms are close to the pristine beaches of the Karpaz peninsula.

✉ Rizokarpaso village, North Cyprus ☎ 372 2009;
www.karpazarchhouses.com

Londa Hotel (€€€)

This sleek contemporary boutique hotel brings Italian style to Limassol. The light, airy feel is consistent throughout the property, and the bar and restaurant attract a faithful local clientele.

✉ 72 Georgiou I, Limassol ☎ 2586 5555; www.londahotel.com

The Mill Hotel (€€)

This former mill is your best accommodation bet in Kakopetria (and the Troodos), both for its large, handsome rooms and its delightfully rustic restaurant upstairs.

✉ 8 Milos, Kakopetria ☎ 2292 2536; www.cymillhotel.com

Salamis Bay Conti Resort (€€€)

Large impressive complex on a fine beach close to the ruins of ancient Salamis. All the facilities you would expect of a 5-star hotel.

✉ Salamis Bay ☎ 378 8200; www.salamisbayconti.com

Off the beaten track

Akamas's gorges

A few companies, including Exalt Travel of Pafos (tel: 2694 3803; www.exalttravel.com), run tours through the gorges, the Avakas being the favourite. It is quite an adventure, negotiating the boulder-strewn river bed with sheer cliffs on either side. If the weather is, or is likely to be bad, avoid the gorges – flash floods here can be dangerous.

Avdimou Coast

Drive to Avdimou Beach (▶ 109), about 30km (18.5 miles) west of Limassol, but take the gravel track to Melanda Beach Taverna, not the road to Avdimou Beach to the east. The beach is often deserted but the clifftop path running west is a delight, with wonderful views over the coastal strip, and leads to the high cliffs above Pissouri Beach. There is, however, no need to go more than 200m (220yds) to find solitude. Occasionally Royal Air Force fighter jets perform spectaclar manoeuvres offshore.

Cedar Valley

This is best reached from Pafos or Limassol. The bitumen road is excellent although narrow in places. The valley is 12km (7.5 miles) away, and at 400m (1,312ft) above sea level, under the canopy of trees, the air is cool. The cedars are magnificent and the stillness is only likely to be disturbed by a moufflon (wild sheep) or the trickle of water from a spring.

Famagusta Bay
The stretch of coast starting about 9km (5.5 miles) north of Protaras has some fine clifftop walks. Access is not entirely obvious. Once on the low escarpments all is straightforward, a bonus being the view of crumbling Famagusta (Gazimağusa; ➤ 166–171) – take binoculars if not planning to visit the North.

Karpasia (Karpaz) Peninsula
Much of northern Cyprus is lovely, but the Karpasia Peninsula is beautiful. Locals go about their business giving you a taste of traditional life you won't experience elsewhere. Take a map and set off on a journey of exploration, stopping at any beach or village that attracts your attention.

Mandria Shore
Turn into Mandria village, east of the road to Pafos airport. Follow the beach signs to Pasa Church and after 500m (545yds) you will reach a T-junction. Go left for another 500m (545yds) and turn right to reach the shore after 1km (0.5 miles), with its shingle beach.

Petounda Point
Take the road west of Kiti village towards Petounda Point for about 6km (3.5 miles). Turn left at the sign for Panagia Petounda Church and after about 1.5km (1 mile) you will see the church on the right, but keep left to reach the shore. There are two houses, but a short walk to the west brings isolation.

Pomos Point to Kato Pyrgos
This section of coast, northeast of Polis in the west, sees fewer visitors than others in the south. Several stretches of dark sand line the various bays and coves. The further east you go the quieter it is. Here the Troodos Mountains descend dramatically to the sea. In the event of a sudden influx of tourist buses there is the opportunity to retreat quickly into the quiet hills.

Interesting diversions

View the forbidden suburb of Varosha at Famagusta (Gazimağusa) through binoculars from the roof of an enterprising Greek Cypriot's house in Deryneia (➤ 91). There is a small charge.

Walk the boards at Harmony Park, Limassol (Lemesos). A 6km (3.5-mile) shore walk has been built westwards from San Raphael Marina. All of it runs close to the water's edge but the central timber section is especially cool and pleasant.

Walk the Green Line in the walled city of Nicosia. The Green Line has lost some of its sting since the opening of the border in 2003, but it still exists and still exerts a peculiar fascination.

Visit the Keo distillery and winery in Limassol at 1 Leoforos Fragklinou Rousvelt (tel: 2585 3100; www.keogroup.com).

Walk a gorge in the Akamas. Exalt Travel in Pafos (tel: 2694 3803), will arrange a guided excursion.

Hire a pedalo on Agia Napa beach and paddle through the unusual weathered rock formations at the east end of the bay.

Take a 2- or 3-day boat trip from Limassol to Israel and Egypt. Local travel agents will provide all details. Try Louis Cruise Lines in Limassol (tel: 2557 0000).

Visit the Grivas Museum on the beach near Chlorakas and see the wooden ship, *Agios Georgios*, used for gunrunning during the EOKA campaign.

See the sunrise over the Pentadaktylos Mountains from the Mesaoria (central plain). Spectacular effects reward a spectacularly early start.

Watch the vultures on Mount Pentadaktylos (Beşparmak, east of Keryneia/Girne). Drive to the pass, but go at the weekend when the nearby quarry is closed.

Exploring

In the south there are 340km (211 miles) of coast to explore, along with the fascinating Troodos Mountains and the towns of Larnaka (Larnaca), Limassol (Lemesos), Pafos (Paphos) and Nicosia (Lefkosia). Visitors in the north have to be content with long unspoiled shores, including the fabled Karpasia Peninsula and the magnificent Pentadaktylos (Beşparmak) Mountains. The extensive Mesaoria plain is there for good measure.

The Cypriots have long had a reputation for being friendly and welcoming. This extra special reception is no longer common in the busy resorts and perhaps will soon be lost for ever, but it can still catch you unawares in a mountain village or the old quarter of Nicosia.

Larnaka and the Southeast

Larnaka

This part of Cyprus was once the agricultural heartland and it still provides the bulk of the Cypriot potato crop, which thrives in the distinctive red soil. However, in the last 20 years the agricultural industry has been supplanted by tourism, focused on two, previously quiet, resorts – Agia Napa and Protaras. The growth of these areas has been dramatic.

Beaches are the main attraction of this region, and the coastline offers a good range of places worth stopping at, although crowds tend to descend on summer weekends. The other attractions of the area are more low key: some traditional villages, Larnaka (Larnaca), the largest town, and a glimpse of the formerly 'forbidden city' of Famagusta (Gazimağusa).

LARNAKA (LARNACA)

Larnaka is a significant tourist and commercial centre and is a convenient base for exploring the island, though its own places of interest are fairly limited. The modern city is built on the remains of ancient Kition, which was, according to the legend, established by one of Noah's grandsons in the 13th century BC. Out of this settlement Larnaka became an important trading centre, from where the island's main export of copper was shipped, and it has long had a large foreign population.

The town can be very busy at rush hour and the narrow streets and one-way system do not help the foreign driver. Visitors should try to park quickly and explore on foot. The pedestrianized seafront is lined with cafés and at the northern end of the promenade is a large marina with berths for 450 yachts. Larnaka is the main yachting centre of the island and the port facilities here attract boats from all over the eastern Mediterranean. There is a very popular beach, but it is man-made and is certainly not among the best on Cyprus. The seafront road provides amenities for tourists with an abundance of cafés, restaurants and ice-cream sellers.

Larnaka has a long history, but much of the evidence has been covered by the modern city. However the enthusiastic will be able to track down archaeological remains and a few historic churches.

 11D

Agios Lazaros Church

Legend states that St Lazarus, having been raised from the dead by Christ, came to Larnaka to live out the rest of his days and when he finally died he was buried here. His remains, however, were stolen and only his empty tomb is visible in the south apse. The church was built in the 9th century and restored in the

17th century, including the decoration of its extremely ornate interior. There is a small museum inside the building.

🚩 *Larnaka 3d* ✉ Odos Agiou Lazarou ☎ Museum: 2465 2498 🕐 Museum: Mon, Tue, Thu, Fri 8:30–12:30, 3–5:30; Wed, Sat 8:30–1; Sun closed. Church: Apr–Sep daily 8–12:30, 3:30–6:30; Oct–May daily 8:30–12:30; 2:30–5 ✋ Museum: inexpensive

Archaeological Museum

This museum has a good collection of exhibits – some date back to 3000BC – from Kition (▶ 88) and Choirokoitia (▶ 110). The first room contains statues and terracotta figurines. The pottery collection occupies the second room, along with some Mycenaean vases. Other rooms contain neolithic items, including a reconstruction of a tomb, and finally some Roman glassware. The garden has fragments of statues and a mosaic pavement.

🚩 *Larnaka 3e* ✉ Odos Kalograion ☎ 2430 4169 🕐 Mon–Fri 9–5. Closed 1 Jan, afternoons Jul–Aug, 25 Dec ✋ Inexpensive 🍴 Cafés nearby (€)

Kition

The remains of the ancient city can be found at a number of sites. The most visible ruins are on Leontiou Machaira near the Archaeological Museum. The ditches and walls date from the 12th and 13th centuries BC, when they enclosed the city. It is also possible to make out the traces of a Phoenician temple, and the sharp eyed may detect images of ships carved into the south wall.

✚ *Larnaka 3e* ✉ Odos Leontiou Machaira 🕐 Mon–Fri 9–5. Closed afternoons Jul–Aug, 1 Jan and 25 Dec 💰 Inexpensive

Larnaka Fort and Medieval Museum

The fort was built in 1625 by the Turks to defend the city against raiders but was soon adapted for use as a prison. It now contains a small medieval museum, featuring mainly suits of armour. There

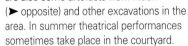

are also some artefacts from Kition (➤ opposite) and other excavations in the area. In summer theatrical performances sometimes take place in the courtyard.

🕇 *Larnaka 3d* ✉ Larnaka seafront, south end of Odos Ankara ☎ 2430 4576 🕔 Jul–Aug Mon–Fri 9–7:30; Sep–May Mon–Fri 9–5. Closed 1 Jan, 25 Dec 🖐 Inexpensive 🍴 Cafés and tavernas nearby (€€)

Pierides Foundation Museum

This museum was founded in 1974 to house the private collection of antiquities of Demetrios Pierides, covering the neolithic period to the Middle Ages. The collection of 3,600 exhibits is displayed

in the Pierides family's fine 19th-century house, and contains early pottery decorated with various designs, items from the site at Marion, mainly jugs and vases, and one of the most important collections of Roman

glassware and jewellery in Europe. The main hall has some early maps of Cyprus and traditional folk artefacts.

🕇 *Larnaka 3d* ✉ Odos Zinonos Kitieos ☎ 2481 4555 🕔 Mon–Thu 9–4, Fri, Sat 9–1. Closed 1 Jan, 25 Dec, Greek Orthodox Easter Sun 🖐 Moderate 🍴 Cafés nearby (€)

More to see in the Southeast

AGIA NAPA

This major resort stretching along the coast has a reputation for clubs and bars. The town centre retains some appeal with its monastery and adjoining square, and the beaches are excellent, but crowded in summer.

Agia Napa Monastery and its gardens are a welcome haven. Its church was built in the 16th century over a cave where an icon of the Virgin Mary was supposedly found. Within a century the monastery had grown rich, owning much land. It was abandoned in the 18th century but later restored under British rule.

The exhibits at the **Tornarites-Pierides Marine Life Museum** include a large number of fossils and shells from Cyprus's waters. A reconstruction of the seabed displays turtles and sharks. One section features marine fauna of the late Cretaceous period and even shows dinosaurs.

Among the sculptures, engravings, vases and ceramics at the **Thalassa Municipal Museum of the Sea** is a full-size replica of the ancient ship *Kyrenia 2* and a papryrus vessel of 9200BC. The museum also has art exhibits and hosts concerts.

✚ 22G

Monastery

✉ Centre of Agia Napa village ◷ Daily ✋ Free 🍴 Many cafés nearby (€€)

Tornarites-Pierides Marine Life Museum

✉ 25 Odos Agias Mavris
☎ 2372 3409
◷ Mon–Wed, Fri, Sat 9–2; Tue 9–2, 3–6 ✋ Moderate
🍴 Many cafés nearby (€€)

Thalassa Municipal Museum of the Sea

✉ Town Square ☎ 2381 6366 ◷ Tue–Wed, Fri, Sat 9–2; Tue 9–2, 3–6
✋ Moderate 🍴 Café

DERYNEIA

If you're not going to visit the North, this town gives an insight into recent Cypriot history. It is the nearest settlement to Famagusta and one villager has set up a viewing point where tourists, for a small fee, can climb up to the roof of his house and look through a telescope across to the closed Famagusta suburb of Varosha.

✚ 21H ✉ 11km (7 miles) north of Agia Napa 🍴 Café in village (€), many restaurants on road to Paralimni (€€) 🚌 From Protaras, in summer every hour 8–3, Sun last bus 1:30

HALA SULTAN TEKKE AND SALT LAKE

Best places to see, ➤ 40–41.

NISSI BEACH

Nissi Beach is where tourist development in this area started. It is a

pleasant sandy beach, though it can be very crowded in summer, with a rocky island just offshore. The presence of a sand bar makes it possible to wade to the island, an adventure that appeals especially to children. Those going to the island should, however, bear in mind that it is made up of rough and spiky rocks and suitable footwear is necessary.

✚ 21G 🖂 2km (1 mile) west of Agia Napa 🍴 Several cafés (€)

PANAGIA ANGELOKTISTI (KITI CHURCH)

Angeloktisti, which means 'built by angels', was constructed in the 11th century on the remains of a 5th-century basilica. It has many ornate icons but its main attraction is a rare 6th-century mosaic that depicts angels attending the Virgin Mary as she holds Christ; it is a very intricate composition, of a style not found elsewhere in Cyprus. The mosaic will be lit up for visitors on request.

✚ 11C 🖂 Edge of the village on road to Mazotos ☎ 2442 4646 🕓 Daily 8–12, 2–4. If locked ask for the key at the nearby café 🖐 Donation requested 🍴 Café nearby (€) 🚌 From Larnaka

POTAMOS TOU LIOPETRI

This pleasant creek serves as a small fishing harbour. At the shoreline there are tavernas and a long, if slightly rocky, beach with the church of Agios Georgios at its western end. Early in the morning, when the fishermen are returning with their catch, it is a lovely place. The beach is usually quiet and provides an opportunity for calm, safe swimming.

✚ 21G 🖂 14km (8.5 miles) west of Agia Napa 🍴 Tavernas on beach (€€)

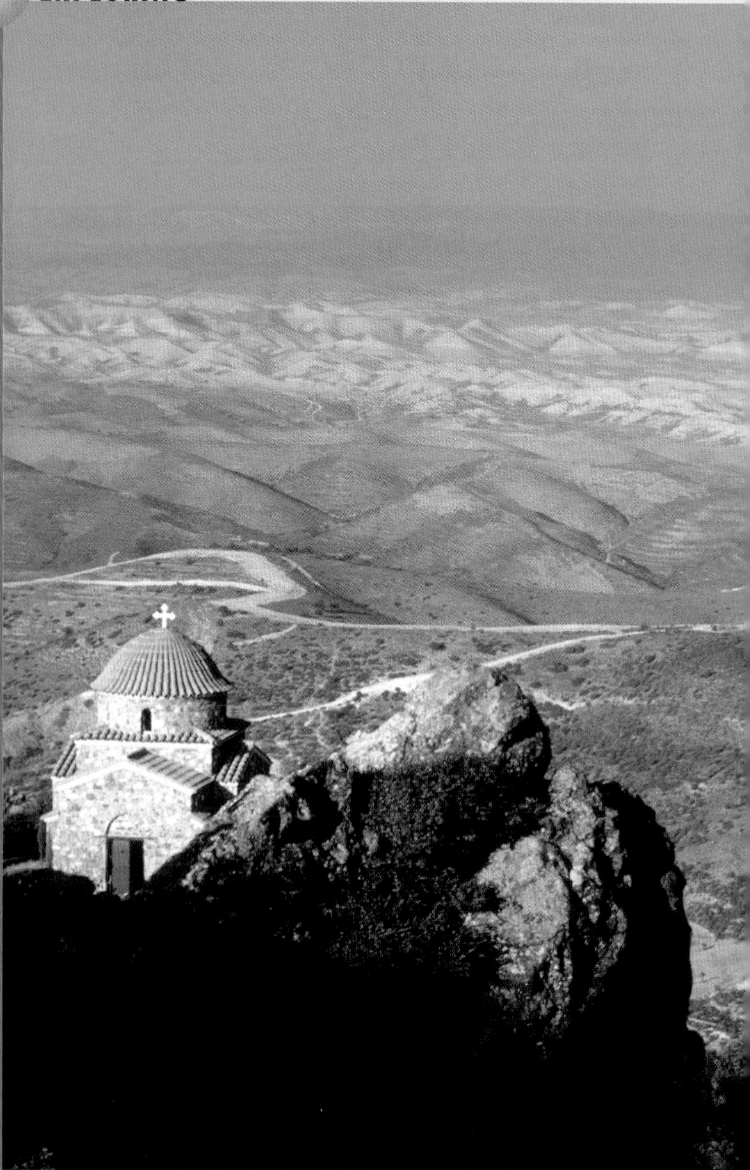

PROTARAS

Protaras, also known as Fig Tree Bay because of a fig tree that was once its only landmark, is a fully fledged resort full of hotels, restaurants and dance clubs. The beach is sandy and there are good water-sports facilities. The offshore rocky islet offers the chance of some small degree of seclusion although you have to be a fairly strong swimmer to reach it.

✚ 22H ✉ 8km (5 miles) north of Cape Gkreko (Greco) on east coast 🍴 Numerous cafés and restaurants (€–€€) 🚌 From Agia Napa in summer: every hour 9–5, Sun 10–5

STAVROVOUNI MONASTERY

The monastery of Stavrovouni, at an altitude of 690m (2,263ft), has spectacular views from the top of the hill. There has been a religious community here since AD327 when St Helena brought a fragment of the True Cross from Jerusalem. It is claimed that the piece is still in the monastery, covered by a silver casing. The original buildings were destroyed by Arab and Turkish raiders and those visible today date mainly from the 17th century. They are still occupied by a devout community of monks, and women are not allowed inside.

✚ 10C ✉ 40km (25 miles) west of Larnaka 🕓 Men only. Apr–Aug daily 8–11, 3–8; Sep–Mar daily 7:30–11, 2–7 ✋ Free

HOTELS

AGIA NAPA

Aeneas (€€€)

The hotel is close to the beach of Nissi Bay. Low-rise buildings surround a large swimming lagoon set among pleasant gardens.

✉ Leoforos Nissi ☎ 2372 4000; www.aeneas.com.cy

The Dome Beach Hotel (€€)

A large four-star hotel overlooking two beaches. Lush gardens surround a good-sized swimming pool.

✉ Makronissos ☎ 2372 1006; www.domehotel.com.cy

Faros (€)

Exceedingly good location for the town and harbour and away from the busiest roads. The rooms are good and the central pool area is excellent.

✉ Leoforos Archiepiskopou Makariou III ☎ 2381 6100; www.faroshotel.com.cy

Grecian Bay (€€)

Directly overlooking the sands of the bay, this hotel has a wide choice of facilities including poolside dining and cool mimosa gardens.

✉ 32 Leoforos Kryou ☎ 2384 2000; www.grecian.com.cy

Nissi Beach (€€)

The first hotel to be built at this wonderful little bay, it stands at the edge of the golden sands. The facilities are extensive.

✉ Leoforos Nissi ☎ 2372 1021; www.nissi-beach.com

Olympic Lagoon Resort (€€)

The hotel is west of the town, built around a lagoon of rocky waterfalls and whirlpools. It is 100m (110yds) to the beach.

✉ Xylophagou–Agía Napa road 3km (2 miles) to resort centre
☎ 2372 2500; www.kanikahotels.com

LARNAKA

Cactus (€)
A family-run hotel with simple but smart rooms and friendly staff.
✉ 6–8 Odos Tyrimou ☎ 2462 7400

Lordos Beach (€€)
On the shores of Larnaka Bay, north of town, this resort hotel with pool and its own small beach has sea-facing balconies.
✉ Dhekelia Road ☎ 2464 7444; www.lordos.com.cy

Louis Princess Beach (€€)
The complex has an international feel. Its 138 rooms are arranged around a good-sized pool and terraces. Next to the beach.
✉ Dhekelia Road, 7km (4 miles) from the town ☎ 2464 5500; www.louishotels.com

Sun Hall (€)
Close to the town beach and well placed for exploring old Larnaka. The outdoor swimming pool is heated in the chillier months.
✉ 6 Leoforos Athinon ☎ 2465 3341; www.sunhallhotel-24.com

PROTARAS

Pallini (€)
These hotel apartments may be basic, but they are right on splendid Fig Tree Bay and near the town.
✉ Fig Tree Bay ☎ 2283 1900

Pernera Beach (€€)
A good retreat by a small beach, midway between Protaras and Paralimni (about 3 km/2 miles to each).
✉ Pernera ☎ 2383 1011; www.pernera.com.cy

RESTAURANTS

AGIA NAPA

Hokkaido (€€)
Japanese food of a high standard. Well designed interior.
✉ 35 Odos Agias Mavris ☎ 2372 1505 🕐 Daily

Limelight Taverna (€€)

One of a handful of local tavernas that have maintained a reputation for authentic Greek dishes and grills.

✉ Odos Liperti ☎ 2372 1650 🕓 Daily

Pagoda (€€)

It may be part of a chain, but Pagoda serves up excellent, authentic Chinese food in a stylish atmosphere. Reservations recommended during summer.

✉ 29 Leoforos Nissi ☎ 2381 9988 🕓 Daily

Vassos (€€)

Popular with locals and visitors alike, and rightly so, thanks to its generous servings of excellent seafood. Right at the harbour.

✉ Agia Napa harbour ☎ 2372 1884 🕓 Daily

LARNAKA

1900 Art Cafe (€€)

Sophisticated local cuisine, home-baked sweets and dried herbs in a restored old house with antique furnishings and modern art.

✉ 6 Odos Stasinou ☎ 2465 3027 🕓 Daily 6–12

Ammos (€)

The white wooden furniture, sunbeds and hammocks give this place a light, summery feel, which is well matched by the fresh, healthy cuisine.

✉ Mackenzie Beach ☎ 2482 8844 🕓 Daily

Habibi (€)

Expect delicious, great-value *meze* (Arabic-style) at this lively Lebanese eatery, and belly-dancing shows on weekends.

✉ 7 Efesou ☎ 7000 3222 🕓 Daily

Militzis (€€)

This traditional taverna, with its stone walls and checked table cloths, is the place to head for Cypriot specialties.

✉ Piale Pasa ☎ 2465 5867 🕓 Daily

To Paradosiako (€)
Popular with the locals, this waterfront venue is one of Larnaka's best-value tavernas, serving up hearty, reasonably priced Cypriot and Greek dishes.

✉ 2 Sakaria, Mackenzie Beach ☎ 2465 8318 🕑 Daily

Varoshiotis Seafood (€€)
Part of a popular family-owned Cypriot chain, all of which serve consistently fresh, generously sized seafood dishes. The waterfront location is a bonus.

✉ Piale Pasa ☎ 7777 7708 🕑 Daily

PROTARAS
Spartiatis (€€)
A bright, modern taverna that hasn't lost its touch with traditional Cypriot fare, Spartiatis has a fine sea view and complements it with seafood fresh from the nearby harbour.

✉ 79 Konnos Beach ☎ 2383 1386 🕑 Daily

Yianna Marie (€€)
Serves breakfast, lunch and dinner and all are rather good. The location is marvellous, set just back from the beach.

✉ Fig Tree Bay, north end ☎ 2381 4440 🕑 Daily

Umi (€€)
The sushi may be exquisite but the sea views alone from this stylish fourth-floor restaurant make it worth dining here.

✉ Grecian Park Hotel ☎ 2384 4044 🕑 Daily, dinner only

SOTIRA
To Ploumin (€€)
It would be hard to find more authentic country-style food than at this rambling 1930s farmhouse decked out with old family photographs, rusty farming implements and antiques. You can dine in the courtyard in summer.

✉ 3 Odos Oktovriou 28 ☎ 2373 0444 🕑 Daily

SHOPPING

JEWELLERY SHOPS

Infinity
Well-designed glass and silver items. Lacework, too.
✉ In front of Trizas Hotel, Fig Tree Bay, Protaras ☎ 2383 1989

SOUVENIR, HANDICRAFTS AND LEATHER

Laiki Geitonia (traditional quarter) at the south end of Odos Zinonos Kitieos has a few shops of interest, although type and ownership change often. About 750m (820yds) to the south on Odos Boz Kourt and Odos Ak Nteniz are some pottery shops.

Athos Icons
Splendid icons along with Byzantine church music, wine and incense, all from Athos Monastery.
✉ 39 Grigoris Afxentiou, Larnaka ☎ 2462 6256

Cyprus Handicraft Service
This Ministry of Commerce and Industry shop has traditional Cypriot crafts: Lefkara lace, silverware, woven cotton, baskets etc.
✉ 6 Odos Kosma Lysioti, Larnaka ☎ 2430 4327

Emira Pottery
Handmade pots of all types and sizes. They also take orders.
✉ 13 Odos Mehmet Ali, Larnaka ☎ 2462 3952

Fotoni's Pottery
✉ 28 Boz Kourt, Larnaka ☎ 2465 0304

Kornos village
Terracotta pottery is produced here as it was 2,000 years ago.

Liopetri and Xylofagou villages
Traditional basket-making.

The Oak Tree Wine Cellar
One of the island's best wine shops, with an extensive range of
Cypriot wines, this is the place to head for liquid souvenirs.
✉ 99G Odos Drousioti, Larnaka ☎ 2481 5044

STORES AND ARCADES
Debenhams
A store selling everything, including records, jewellery and lingerie.
It also has a food hall and a bookshop.
✉ Leoforos Stratigou Timayia, Larnaka ☎ 2463 1111

ENTERTAINMENT AND SPORT

CULTURAL EVENTS
Agia Napa Festival (September)
In front of the monastery, with folk music and dancing.
✉ Agia Napa ☎ 2381 6307

Larnaka Festival (July)
Dance, theatre, music, cinema, and poetry performances at the
fort and the Patticheion Municipal Theatre.
✉ Larnaka ☎ 2465 7745

HORSEBACK RIDING
Moonshine Ranch
✉ Kavo Gkreko Road, opposite Grecian Bay Hotel, Agia Napa
☎ 9960 5042

SAILING
Larnaka Marina
Facilities for visiting yachts.
✉ Larnaka ☎ 2465 3110

TEN-PIN BOWLING
Rock 'n' Bowl
✉ Odos Dhekelia, Larnaka ☎ 2482 2777 🕐 11am–midnight

Limassol and the Southwest

This region has something for all tastes and all interests: an attractive coastline, a medieval castle, spectacular views, archaeological sites and, for the mythologically or romantically inclined, the birthplace of Aphrodite.

Limassol (Lemesos)

Anyone interested in history will find plenty to occupy them. The 9,000-year-old site at Choirokoitia is the oldest settlement on the island, while Kourion and its restored amphitheatre has relics from the Mycenaean, Persian and Roman periods. There are links with mythology too – a temple to Apollo – and, at Petra tou Romiou, the place where Aphrodite is said to have emerged from the foaming sea. A newer tradition, only 500 years old, is found in the lacemaking village of Lefkara, and beyond Limassol (Lemesos) are the vital ingredients for any Cypriot holiday, some good beaches.

LIMASSOL (LEMESOS)

Limassol's main claim to fame is that England's Richard the Lionheart was shipwrecked here and married his fiancée Berengaria in the town. The Knights Hospitaller developed Limassol as a trading post based on export of the Commandaria wine, which they made from the vineyards surrounding Kolossi. However, it was only in the 19th century that its major asset, the deep-water port, began to be appreciated and the town became a significant commercial centre.

In recent years Limassol has seen massive tourist development along the wide and noisy approach road on a stretch of coast without good beaches. It is a modern town but it does not lack atmosphere and has good shopping, nightlife and restaurants. The carnival in spring and the wine festival in early September are particularly lively times to visit the town.

The sights of Limassol are easily explored on foot, indeed cars will encounter traffic problems and a fiendish one-way system. The main historical sight is the castle and medieval museum. There are also a couple of mosques – reminders of Limassol's Turkish quarter. The main shopping area is around Odos Agiou Andreou.

✚ 7B

Amathous

These archaeological remains are spread widely and include a rock-cut tomb in the grounds of the Amathus Beach hotel. The most easily accessible ruins are of the Agora, in a fenced site just off the main road on the inland side. This was the market area and though it is a relatively small site many pillars are still visible, which make it quite an impressive place. Up a track from the Agora is the Acropolis and remains of a Temple to Aphrodite. There is evidence that some of the site lies underwater, which offers interesting opportunities for snorkellers and scuba-divers.

✚ 8B ✉ 8km (5 miles) east of Limassol 🕓 Apr–May, Sep–Oct daily 9–6; Jun–Aug daily 9–7:30; Nov–Mar daily 9–5 ✋ Inexpensive 🚌 From Limassol and Larnaka

Castle and Cyprus Medieval Museum

The main buildings of the castle were constructed in the 14th century on the site of an earlier Byzantine fortification. The chapel in which Richard the Lionheart and Berengaria were married was part of the original castle but is no longer standing. The castle was occupied by the Turks and later used by the British as an army headquarters.

The Cyprus Medieval Museum is now housed here. The basement contains replicas of sculptures and photographs of the Byzantine churches of Cyprus. Upstairs the exhibits are in small rooms off a central hall, with the most memorable items – armour and weapons – on the second floor. The final flight of

stairs leads out on to the battlements, from where there are good views of the city. The most distinctive sights on the skyline are the two mosques, Cami Djedid and Cami Kebir, reminders that this was once the Turkish part of town.

✚ *Limassol 2a* ✉ Odos Eirinis, near the old harbour ☎ 2530 5419 ⏲ Mon–Sat 9–5, Sun 10–1. Closed 1 Jan, 25 Dec 🖐 Moderate 🍴 Many cafés nearby (€)

District Archaeological Museum

The garden contains a sundial that supposedly belonged to the British Lord Kitchener. Inside, Room 1 contains neolithic tools and pottery from Amathous (➤ 104) and Kourion (➤ 42–43). These artefacts are very old, with some dating back to 2300BC. Room 2 has later figurines and Roman coins. The final room contains statues from Amathous, including those of Artemis and the Egyptian god Bes.

✚ *Limassol 4c* ✉ Corner of Odos Kanningos and Odos Vyronos ☎ 2530 5157 ⏲ Mon–Fri 10–5, Sat 10–1. Closed 1 Jan, 25 Dec, Greek Orthodox Easter Sun 🖐 Moderate

Municipal Gardens and Zoo

The Municipal Gardens provide some welcome greenery in a dusty city. They also contain a small zoo, though the animals are kept in poor conditions. There is a small open-air theatre, where productions are held during the summer. The gardens are also the site of the annual Limassol Wine Festival, held in September. All the local wine companies set up stalls and have an evening of free wine tasting accompanied by music and dancing.

✚ *Limassol 4c* ✉ Odos Oktovriou 28 ☎ 2558 8345 ◷ Gardens: daylight hours. Zoo: daily 9–6:30 ✋ Gardens: free. Zoo: moderate 🍴 Café in the Gardens (€)

More to see in the Southwest

AKROTIRI PENINSULA

The area contains a dark sand beach, a salt lake and a historic church. In summer the salt lake is dry, has a grey colour and you can smell the salt; in winter it fills with water and is a stopping off point for passing flamingos. Lady's Mile Beach is sandy and has safe swimming in the shallow sea. The far end is closed off, marking the start of the British base at Akrotiri – the occasional military jet may disturb the peace.

The monastery of **Agios Nikolaos ton Gaton** (St Nicholas of the Cats) is reached on a track at the southern end of the beach. It was founded in AD325, though the buildings seen today were constructed in the 13th century and have been restored since. The cats in the name are still much in evidence.

✚ 6A

Agios Nikolaos ton Gaton

🕐 Daily 🆓 Free 🍴 Cafés on beach (€), open summer only

AVDIMOU BEACH

Avdimou Beach is a good long sandy stretch, though the water becomes deep very quickly. There is a small taverna at each end separated by a headland and it is usually quiet, but at weekends it can be busy with service personnel and their families.

✚ 5A ✉ 3km (2 miles) off main road 🍴 Tavernas on beach (€)

CHOIROKOITIA

This is the oldest archaeological site on the island, dating from 6800BC when 2,000 people lived here and farmed the surrounding land.

The stone houses that define the settlement come in two sizes, one about 4m (13ft) across and the other 8m (26ft). They were built close together and linked by narrow passageways, and it was apparently crowded. The inhabitants tended to bury their dead under the floor of the house and then build on top. Some houses have revealed up to eight different periods of occupation.

The settlement is best explored by following the vestiges of the

main street, with House A near the entrance being the easiest to make out. A second group of ruins has the remains of pillars visible, which once supported the roof. From there the site becomes more complicated and the best views are from the top of the hill, from where the wider perspective can reveal its layout. Be warned though: there are lots of stairs.

➕ 9C ✉ Off Junction 14 Nicosia–Limassol motorway ☎ 2432 2710
🕐 Apr–May, Sep–Oct daily 9–6; Jun–Aug Mon–Fri 9–7:30, Sat–Sun 9–5; Nov–Mar daily 9–5. Closed 1 Jan, 25 Dec, Greek Orthodox Easter Sun
💷 Inexpensive

GOVERNOR'S BEACH

See page 68.

KOLOSSI CASTLE

Kolossi was the headquarters of the Knights Hospitaller, who built the first castle in the late 13th century. They exploited the land here, using local sugar and grapes to make Commandaria wine.

The castle suffered from a number of attacks by Egyptian Mameluke raiders in the 14th century, and the buildings visible today date from a rebuilding that took place in the 15th century. The Turks took it over in 1570 and sugar production continued until 1799. Visitors pass over a drawbridge into a pleasant garden and then into the keep, which has a thick wall and rises to three storeys.

Much of the ground floor was used as a storage area. The first floor has two large rooms and a kitchen. On the top floor were the apartments of the Grand Commander. A spiral staircase leads on to the roof, from where there are good views.

✚ 6B ✉ 14.5km (9 miles) from Limassol ☎ 2593 4907 ⏱ Apr–May, Sep–Oct daily 9–6; Jun–Aug daily 9–7:30; Nov–Mar daily 8–5 ✋ Inexpensive 🍽 Cafés nearby (€–€€)

KOURION

Best places to see, ➤ 42–43.

LEFKARA

The village is divided into Pano (upper) and Kato (lower) Lefkara, and is a very popular tourist destination. Visitors who prefer to avoid the crowds come in the early morning.

Lefkara is known for its lace, called *lefkaritika*; it first became famous in 1481 when Leonardo da Vinci supposedly ordered some for Milan Cathedral. The lace then became popular with Venetian ladies and the lacemaking industry took off. The tradition continues to flourish and rather ferocious ladies will offer their wares vigorously to passing tourists. Those wishing to buy should take care to ensure that it is the genuine article and not imported. There are also a number of silverware shops.

The main street of Pano Lefkara is now designed to cater for tourists but the narrow alleys to either side are still peaceful places to wander. There is also a small **museum** of lacemaking and silverware, signposted uphill from the main street.

The lower half of the village has been renovated and is worth a visit. Its church of the Archangel Michael has some beautiful 18th-century icons and there are good views across the hills from outside the building. The distinctive houses in this part of the village are painted blue and white and its streets are extremely narrow and fairly traffic free.

➕ 9C ✉ 9km (5.5 miles) northwest of junction 13 of the Nicosia–Limassol motorway 🍴 Cafés in the main street of the upper and lower villages (€)

Museum
☎ 2434 2326 🕐 Mon–Thu 9:30–4, Fri–Sat 10–4
✋ Inexpensive

PETRA TOU ROMIOU (ROCK OF APHRODITE)

This is one of the most photographed sites on the whole island. The name means the Rock of Romios and the two large rocks in the sea, set against the white cliffs, provide a spectacular scene. There are two official places to stop – one close to the rock, just back from the shore, where there is a kiosk and a car park, the other higher up in the cliffs, where there is a tourist pavilion and restaurant. However, the best view, coming from Limassol, is on the final bend before the road starts to descend; a parking bay on the left makes a convenient stopping place.

Legend states that this was the birthplace of Aphrodite, where she emerged from the water. The beach itself is shingly, and it is not ideal for swimming because it gets rough around the rocks, but it is worth stopping to soak up the mystical atmosphere.

✚ 3B ✉ 24km (15 miles) east of Pafos 🍴 Café in the tourist pavilion (€)

SANCTUARY OF APOLLO YLATIS

The temple was first used in the 8th century BC, though the present ruins date from AD100, when it was rebuilt after an earthquake. There is a waymarked path and map to guide the visitor around the site. The circular remains of a votive pit are worth a closer look. The pit was used to store unwanted ritual gifts, and archaeologists have found it a rich source of artefacts. The path then leads to the Temple of Apollo, which has been partially restored, its high columns a striking reminder of ancient times. A sleek new structure covers the Priest's House where you can see some mosaics and pillars.

The remaining buildings of interest are the Palaestra, which was an open space used for sporting activities, and a nearby complex of baths and dormitories.

✚ 5B ✉ Limassol–Pafos road ☻ Apr–May, Sep–Oct daily 9–6; Jun–Aug daily 9–7:30; Nov–Mar daily 9–5. Closed 1 Jan, 25 Dec, Greek Orthodox Easter Sun 🖐 Inexpensive

HOTELS

LIMASSOL (LEMESOS)

Atlantica Miramare Beach (€€)

This hotel was built long before Limassol's coastal strip grew into a continuous ribbon of development. It became popular with the British over the years, not least because of the excellent service.
✉ Odos Amerikanas, Potamos Germasogeias ☎ 2588 8100; www.atlanticahotels.com

Amathus Beach (€€€)

Opulent and with fine gardens, the Amathus Beach is situated by the shore at the eastern end of the tourist strip.
✉ Leoforos Amathous ☎ 2583 2000; www.amathushotel.com

Curium Palace (€)

This elegant old hotel has ben renovated to successfully blend a modern look with old-world charm and hospitality. Dining options are first class.
✉ 11 Odos Lordou Vyronou ☎ 2589 1100; www.curiumpalace.com

The Four Seasons (€€€)

See page 76.

Londa Hotel (€€€)

See page 77.

Mediterranean Beach Hotel (€€)

This freshly renovated property on the beach is a good choice for families with its big swimming pools, spa and gym.
✉ Leoforos Amathous ☎ 2531 1777; www.medbeach.com

Le Meridien Limassol Spa & Resort (€€€)

Excellent in every respect, including sumptuous well-planned rooms, splendid indoor and outdoor pools, and lawns that sweep down to the shore. Residents-only operation allows privacy and exclusive use of all facilities.
✉ Leoforos Amathous ☎ 2586 2000; www.lemeridien-cyprus.com

PISSOURI
Bunch of Grapes Inn (€)
A restored old inn set around a pleasant courtyard with 11 simply decorated guest rooms.

✉ 9 Odos Ioannou Erotokritou, Pissouri village ☎ 2522 1275

Columbia Beach Resort (€€€)
See page 76.

Pissouriana Plaza Apartments (€)
Reasonably spacious apartments with spectacular views. There is a big swimming pool.

✉ Pissouri village ☎ 2522 1027; www.pissouriana.com

RESTAURANTS

LIMASSOL (LEMESOS)
Artima (€€)
A popular lunch spot for local businesspeople, this large, stylish Italian restaurant handles all the classics with aplomb.

✉ Carob Mill complex, Odos Vasilissis, opposite Medieval Castle ☎ 2582 0466 🕐 Daily

Barolo (€€€)
With its intimate atmosphere and excellent service this is a delightful place to enjoy some quality modern Mediterranean cuisine and impressive wines.

✉ 248 Odos Agiou Andreou ☎ 2576 0767 🕐 Mon–Sat 7pm–11pm

Beige (€€)
Often touted as the best fine dining in town, Beige offers an oddly eclectic menu in a lovely, romantic room.

✉ 238 Odos Agiou Andreou ☎ 2581 8860 🕐 Mon–Sat dinner only

Caprice (€€€)

The stylish Londa Hotel's signature restaurant serves up cuisine that's every bit as hip as the hotel. Expect Mediterranean cuisine with a twist, a good local wine list and attentive service.

✉ Londa Hotel, 72 Georgiou I ☎ 2586 5555; www.londahotel.com ⏰ Daily, dinner only

Draught (€€–€€€)

An old carob warehouse close to the Cami Kebir mosque has been transformed into a chic casual eatery and microbrewery. It gets busy at weekends and after 10pm.

✉ Odos Vasilissis ☎ 2582 0430 ⏰ Daily

Ladas Old Harbour Fish Restaurant (€€)

The fish comes straight from the boats in the adjacent harbour to this traditional restaurant, which has been here for more than 50 years. It reaches your plate with the minimum of delay.

✉ Old Harbour ☎ 2536 5760 ⏰ Daily

Mavromatis (€€€)

Greek goes gastronomic at this fascinating restaurant that takes simple fare to a higher plane. Excellent service and wine list.

✉ The Four Seasons Hotel, Amathus Leoforos ☎ 2585 8000; www.fourseasons.com.cy ⏰ Mon–Sat, dinner only

La Mer (€)

A good place for lunch if you have just done the Limassol walk (► 72–73).

✉ Elpa Court, Odos Oktovriou 28, just west of Municipal Gardens ☎ 2535 6095 ⏰ Daily

Vivaldi (€€€)

Easily the most inventive and satisfying Italian fare on the island, served in a romantic room with unobtrusive but informed service. Don't expect pizza, but expect surprising twists to Italian classics.

✉ The Four Seasons Hotel, Amathus Leoforos ☎ 2585 8000; www.fourseasons.com.cy ⏰ Tue–Sun, dinner only

PISSOURI
Apollon Taverna (€€)
There's the usual Greek fare during the day, but at night this taverna is known for its magnificent 'Apollon Meze'.

✉ Columbia Beach Resort, Pissouri Bay ☎ 2583 3000; www.columbia-hotels.com ⏱ Daily

Bunch of Grapes Inn (€€)
See page 58.

Flavours of India (€)
For a break from endless village salads, this modest eatery serves honest Indian fare with fine flavoured curries.

✉ Shop 1–2 Ambelonon, Pissouri Bay ☎ 2522 2681 ⏱ Daily

SHOPPING

JEWELLERY
Precious Metal Gallery
Beautifully crafted gold, silver and enamel jewellery.

✉ Shop 17, Agora Anexartisias, Odos Agiou Andreou, Limassol ☎ 2535 3639

SOUVENIRS, LEATHER AND HANDICRAFTS
Artouch
Paintings, sculptures, ceramics and hand-crafted jewellery.

✉ 29 Odos Agiou Andreou, Limassol ☎ 2576 2660

Cyprus Handicraft Service
Good quality Cypriot handicrafts made in Government-run workshops.

✉ 25 Odos Themidos, Limassol ☎ 2530 5118

House of Lace
Large selection of Lefkara lace.

✉ 143 Odos Agiou Andreou, Limassol ☎ 2536 5040

Lefkara Village
A wide range of silverware and lace on sale in the village (➤ 112). Check that you are buying a genuine article, not an import.

Sea Sponge Exhibition Centre
Natural beauty products, including soaps and loofahs, along with seashells and starfish.
✉ Old Port, Limassol ☎ 2535 9933

Stratis Leatherland
✉ 32 Odos Agiou Andreou, Limassol ☎ 2534 5439

STORES AND ARCADES
Agora
An impressive modern arcade. Some quality clothes and footwear outlets along with a jewellery gallery.
✉ Junction of Odos Agiou Andreou and Odos Anexartisias, Limassol

Anexartisia Shopping Street
Has around 160 shops. Although some outlets might close, the Street is here to stay and is worth a visit.
✉ Odos Anexartisias, Limassol

Debenhams
The standard range of department store goods.
✉ 369 Odos Oktovriou 28, Limassol ☎ 2559 1133

Medieval Arcade
Mainly restaurants and cafés, but includes a bookshop.
✉ West end of Odos Agiou Andreou, Limassol

ENTERTAINMENT AND SPORT
CULTURAL EVENTS
Ancient Greek Drama Festival (July–August)
Performances of classical drama are held in the amphitheatre at Kourion and other open-air theatres in the area.

Limassol Festival
Limassol Municipality organizes theatre, music and dance events throughout the summer.
✉ Limassol ☎ 2574 5919

HORSEBACK RIDING
Amathus Park Riding School
✉ Near Parekklisia, Highway junction 21 ☎ 9960 4109

Drapia Farm
✉ Kalavasos, 30km (18.5 miles) east of Limassol ☎ 2433 2998

Elias Country Club
✉ Near Parekklisia, 10km (6 miles) northeast of Limassol ☎ 2563 6000

LAWN BOWLING
Club Aphrodite
✉ 94 Gallias, Erimi ☎ 2593 2488 🕐 Daily 8am–late

SAILING
Cyprus Yachting Association
✉ 21 Amathountos, Limassol ☎ 2532 0599; www.cya.org.cy

Relax Catamaran Cruises
Sailing from Limassol Old Port to Cape Gata; various permutations of time, distance and price.
☎ 8000 8007; 9956 2074; www.relax-cruises.net

St Raphael Marina
Visiting yachtsmen and -women can use the facilities of the St Raphael Hotel marina.
✉ Limassol ☎ 2563 5800

TEN-PIN BOWLING
Space Bowling
✉ 1 Odos Eracleous, motorway junction 23 area, Germasogeia ☎ 2531 0000
🕐 Daily 10am–2am

Pafos and the West

This is the region for those looking for some of Cyprus's quieter and more traditional areas. However, Pafos (Paphos) continues to expand greatly and has cast off its small-town origins, although not its important archaeological heritage. In the north are monasteries and villages. Polis, the only town of any size on the north coast, is no longer as laid-back as it once was. In the far northwest is the Akamas Peninsula, which is the focus of environmental initiatives to protect some of the most remote and beautiful landscapes in Cyprus. East of Polis is an undeveloped region with clean empty beaches, scenic coastline, dramatic mountains and quiet roads up to the North Cyprus border.

Pafos

PAFOS (PAPHOS)

The first settlement dates from the 4th century BC and Pafos played an important role in early Cypriot history. After the 4th century AD it declined and, though its fortunes improved marginally under British administration, it is only in the last 30 years, as transport links improved, that Pafos has seen real growth. Tourist development, in particular, took off after the construction of the international airport in 1983. The richness of its archaeology has qualified ancient Nea Pafos as a UNESCO World Heritage Site.

The town is split into upper and lower Pafos, known as Kitma and Kato Pafos. The lower part, on the coast, contains most of the historic sites, whereas the upper town contains the main commercial centre, shops and museums. It is quite a strenuous walk between the two parts of town. The lower town contains a number of archaeological sites. Some are in formal areas, but you might come across ancient ruins among modern houses. The picturesque harbour is the focus of the lower town and is a pleasant place to stroll. Cafés string out along the seafront and there are plenty of places to eat or have a drink, although it can be very busy at the height of the season.

 2C

Catacombs

There are two underground churches in Pafos. Agia Solomoni is easily identified because those who believe in the magical curative powers of the tomb attach items of clothing to the tree outside.

The underground chambers include a 12th-century chapel with frescoes, some of which are damaged by water and early graffiti by passing crusaders. The chambers are dark and a torch is useful, though the main chapel is lit by candles.

The second catacomb, a few minutes' walk north, is larger, but has been less well cared for.

✚ Pafos 2c ✉ Leoforos Apostolou Pavlou ⏰ Daylight hours ✋ Free

District Archaeological Museum

The museum houses most of the finds from local excavations. In the entrance hall is a Hellenistic sarcophagus from Pegeia, and there are pottery and terracotta figures from Polis. There are also small statues and artefacts from the House of Dionysos, and sculpture and coins from the ancient city kingdoms of Cyprus. Most fascinating are articles found in Room 3, including marble Roman eyeballs and clay hot-water bottles.

✚ Pafos 4d ✉ Leoforos Georgiou Griva Digeni ☎ 2630 6215 ⏰ Mon–Fri 9–4, Sat–Sun 9–1. Closed 1 Jan, 25 Dec, Greek Orthodox Easter Sun ✋ Inexpensive 🍴 Cafés across the road (€)

Ethnographical Museum

The private collection of George Eliades, a local professor, ranges from neolithic to modern times. It includes axe heads, coins, pottery and farm implements from around the island. There is also a reconstruction of a bridal chamber displaying traditional costumes and furniture.

✚ Pafos 3d ✉ 1 Odos Exo Vrisis ☎ 2693 2010 ⏰ Mar–Nov Mon–Sat 9–5, Sun 10–1; Dec–Feb Mon–Sat 9:30–5, Sun 10–1 ✋ Inexpensive 🍴 Cafés nearby (€€)

Odeion

This theatre has been partially restored to give an impression of how it would once have been. It was built in the 2nd century AD, during the Roman period, then suffered earthquake damage in the 7th century and was abandoned. Occasional performances are held here during the summer and details are available from the tourist office. Just in front of the Odeion is the Agora, once the city's marketplace. The foundations and some of the columns survive, and there are remains of some other municipal buildings.

✚ *Pafos 1c* ✉ Within the UNESCO World Heritage-listed Archaeological Park, a short distance inland from the harbour 🕐 Jun–Aug daily 8–7:30; Sep–May daily 8–5 👋 Moderate, including Mosaics (➤ 48–49) and Saranta Kolones (➤ 127) 🍴 Cafés nearby (€)

Pafos Archaeological Park

Best places to see, ➤ 48–49.

Pafos Fort

Originally the harbour was guarded by two castles built by the
Lusignans in the 13th century. Both were badly damaged when
the Turks attacked in 1570, but one was subsequently restored and
used by the Turks as a prison. It is open to the public and you
approach across a drawbridge. The main attractions are the
dungeons and battlements, from where there are excellent views.

✚ *Pafos 1b* ✉ Harbour Wall 🕓 Jun–Aug daily 10–6; Sep–May daily 10–5.
Closed 1 Jan, 25 Dec, Greek Orthodox Easter Sun 🖐 Inexpensive 🍴 Cafés on
harbourfront (€€)

St Paul's Pillar and Agia Kyriaki

This is a small archaeological site in
the back streets of Pafos, where a
large number of columns and other
fragments remain from the early
Christian Basilica of Agia Kyriaki.
Excavations are still taking place and
this may mean that parts of the site
will be closed off. Most people come
here to see St Paul's Pillar, which
stands at the western end of the
site. According to legend, St Paul

was tied to this stone and given 39 lashes as a punishment for
preaching Christianity. Despite this early setback, he later managed
to convert the governor, and the rest of the island soon followed
suit.

The adjacent church of Panagia Chrysopolitissa dates from
the 12th century and is still used for services.

✚ *Pafos 2b* ✉ Odos Stassandrou 🕓 Daylight hours 🖐 Free
🍴 Cafés nearby (€)

Saranta Kolones (Forty Columns) Byzantine Fort

This castle dates from around the 7th century, although it was rebuilt in the 12th century, probably to protect the city from seaborne raiders. The remains of many of the original columns, the central keep and some of the towers on the thick outer walls can still be made out. You can also see a horse trough and ancient latrines. The site is completely open and you can scramble around the ruins, but take care if you have young children.

✚ Pafos 2b ✉ Within the UNESCO World Heritage-listed Pafos Archaeological Park, a short distance from the harbour ☀ Jun–Aug daily 8–7:30; Sep–May daily 8–5 ✋ Moderate, including Mosaics (➤ 48–49) and Odeion (➤ 124) 🍴 Cafés nearby (€€)

Tombs of the Kings (Tafon ton Vasileon)

The 100 tombs on the site cover a wide area and are cut out of the ground with a steep drop into them, so take care when exploring. Steps lead down inside the tombs, often into a whole series of passageways. The chambers near the centre of the site get busy and it is worth walking a little further to those on the edge of the area, which are just as impressive. They are constructed with Doric columns, date from about the 3rd century BC and were probably used to bury members of local noble families.

There are great views over the sea and a few coves are accessible.

✚ Pafos 1e ✉ Leoforos Tafon ton Vasileon, 2km (1 mile) northwest of Pafos ☎ 2630 6295 ☀ Apr–May, Sep–Oct daily 8–6; Jun–Aug daily 8–7:30; Nov–Mar daily 8–5 ✋ Inexpensive 🍴 Cafés nearby (€) 🚌 10, 15 from Pafos

More to see in the West

AGIOS GEORGIOS

Agios Georgios is a pleasant harbour with a handful of restaurants and a small cluster of rooms to rent surrounded by sprawling villa developments. The area was once a Roman settlement and some of the tombs cut out of the rock can be seen. On the headland are the remains of a 6th-century basilica.

The harbour is reached down a track from the headland. It is a very pretty place with a good stretch of sand and a view to the rocky island of Geronisos.

✚ 1D ✉ 25km (15.5 miles) north of Pafos 🍴 Restaurants overlooking the harbour (€)

AGIOS NEOFYTOS MONASTERY

Saint Neofytos set up residence in caves he cut out of the hillside in 1159. The first cave he created was called the *enkleistra*, or enclosure. He then enlarged the dwelling with the addition of three new chambers, which are decorated with religious wall paintings focusing on the Crucifixion and Resurrection. The 16th-century monastery church is dedicated to the Virgin Mary and contains a large number of paintings that depict her early life. Neofytos's bones are also kept here in a wooden sarcophagus, with his skull in a silver reliquary, which the devoted queue up to kiss.

✚ 2C ✉ 9km (5.5 miles) north of Pafos 🕐 Apr–Oct daily 9–12, 2–4; Nov–Mar daily 9–4 👋 Inexpensive 🍴 Café outside monastery (€) 🚌 Two buses a day from Pafos lower town

AKAMAS PENINSULA

Best places to see, ➤ 38–39.

CORAL BAY
See page 68.

GEROSKIPOU

The church of Agia Paraskevi, in the centre of this outer suburb of Pafos, is famous throughout the island because of its distinctive five-domed plan. The building dates from the 10th-century but it has a number of decorations over the altar from the 9th century. The paintings are slightly later, from the 12th to the 15th century.

There is also an impressive Folk Art Museum, just off the main street, which contains farming and domestic implements and traditional costumes. The town is known for its *loukoumi* ('Cyprus delight', called 'Turkish delight' before the Turkish invasion); it is possible to watch it being made in a few shops.

✚ 2B ✉ 3km (2 miles) east of Pafos ☎ Agia Paraskevi: 2696 1859.
Folk Art Museum: 2630 6216 🕐 Church: Apr–Oct Mon–Sat 8–1, 2–5;
Nov–Mar Mon–Sat 8–1, 2–4, Sun 10–1. Folk Art Museum: Apr–Oct daily 9–5;
Nov–Mar daily 8–4 ✋ Church: free. Folk Art Museum: inexpensive 🚌 From Pafos old town

LARA
Best places to see, ➤ 44–45.

PALAIA PAFOS (OLD PAFOS) ARCHAEOLOGICAL SITE AND KOUKLIA LOCAL MUSEUM
The site, on which stands the Sanctuary of Aphrodite, is spread over a large area. There is a restored Lusignan manor (La Covocle)

with substantial and impressive Turkish additions that is now a museum with exhibits focusing on the history of the excavation of the area and the fragments of mosaic that have been found. Its prize possession is a large black stone that stood as a manifestation of Aphrodite and was worshipped by pilgrims. The building itself is worth a closer look as it is one of the best examples of 13th-century Gothic architecture on the island.

To the east of the museum are the Roman remains, including remnants of the Sanctuary of Aphrodite, which stands around a courtyard where rituals took place. The south wing is the best preserved, and parts of the original walls still stand.

West of the sanctuary are the ruins of Roman houses, including the House of Leda; follow the path that leads to a replica of a mosaic of Leda and the Swan.

✚ 3B ✉ 16km (8.5 miles) east of Pafos ☎ 2643 2155 🕐 Daily 9–4. Closed 1 Jan, 25 Dec, Greek Orthodox Easter Sun 🖐 Museum: moderate. Rest of the site: free

PANAGIA CHRYSORROGIATISSA MONASTERY

The monastery is impressive mainly because of its setting at a height of 610m (2,000ft). It was founded in 1152 by a monk called Ignatius, although the main part of the monastery was not built until 1770. These buildings were burned down in 1821 when the Turks suspected the monks of political activity. Further trouble came in the 1950s when the abbot was murdered by EOKA terrorists who thought, erroneously, he had betrayed some of their comrades.

The current abbot has shown much enterprise in reopening an old winery and the monks now produce and sell some excellent wines. A collection of icons and utensils is displayed in an area called the Treasury. Icons, painted by the abbot, are also for sale.

✚ 3D 🖂 3km (2 miles) south of Pano Panagia ☎ 2672 2457
🕐 Daily 9–sunset. Treasury: closed 12:30–1:30 ✋ Free.
Treasury: inexpensive

PANO PANAGIA

This village is the place where Archbishop Makarios
was born. Makarios played a key role in the
campaign for independence from the British and he
was the first president of Cyprus from independence
in 1960 until his death in 1977.

His parents' house in the village is now a museum.
It consists of two rooms, with their bed, assorted
crockery and family photographs. If nothing else, the
house shows that Archbishop Makarios had a humble
background. In the main square is a cultural centre,
which displays more photographs and memorabilia
from his later life as president.

✚ 4D 🖂 Pano Panagia village centre ☎ Cultural centre:
2672 2473. Makarios's House: 2672 2255 🕐 Cultural Centre:
May–Sep daily 9–1, 3–6; Oct–Apr daily 9–1, 2–4. Makarios's
House: daily 9–2, 2–4 ✋ Cultural Centre: free. Makarios's
House: inexpensive 🍴 Cafés in village (€)

POLIS

Once a destination for backpackers and more unconventional travellers, these days Polis attracts a chic set. Most of the main restaurants and shops are found around a pedestrianized square, with a number of rooms and apartments to rent close by. There is a good beach a short walk from the town centre, with a campsite adjacent.

Just east of the town, but difficult to identify, is the ancient site of Marion, which was founded in the 7th century BC and developed into one of the 10 city kingdoms of Cyprus.

✚ 2E ⑪ Cafés in main square (€)

POMOS

There are some wonderful quiet beaches along this section of coast, and as the road climbs up into the cliffs there are amazing views. Just beyond Pomos Point is a small fishing harbour and sheltered beach. Kokkina is occupied by the Turkish army and is inaccessible. The road detours inland and then reaches Kato Pyrgos where there is another isolated beach.

✚ 3F ✉ 22km (13.5 miles) northwest of Polis ⑪ Cafés at Kato Pyrgos and on seafront (€) ▣ Limited bus service from Polis to Pomos, at 11, 2, 4, 6; Sat 11, 2:30, 4

HOTELS

CORAL BAY

Coral Beach Hotel and Resort (€€€)

Large hotel adjacent to the sandy beach at Coral Bay. Facilities include indoor and outdoor swimming pools. The popular beach can get very busy.

✉ Coral Bay ☎ 2688 1000; www.coral.com.cy

PAFOS (PAPHOS)

Agapinor (€)

Old-fashioned but comfortable rooms (73), plus a decent restaurant and coffee shop. Remarkable views.

✉ 24–28 Odos Nikodimou Mylona, Pafos ☎ 2693 3926; www.agapinorhotel.com.cy

Aloe (€€)

This well-run hotel is near the shore and the amenities of Kato Pafos.

✉ Leoforos Poseidonos, Kato Pafos ☎ 2696 4000; www.aloe-hotel.com

Annabelle (€€€)

A renowned luxury hotel in a prime position in town with verdant gardens and an enormous swimming pool.

✉ Leoforos Poseidonos, Kato Pafos ☎ 2693 8333; www.theannabellehotel.com

Atlantica Golden Beach (€€)

A big resort hotel beside a small beach and pretty bay lined with palm trees.

✉ Kissonerga ☎ 2694 7777; www.atlanticahotels.com

Cynthiana Beach (€€)

This elegant hotel has resort facilities and reasonable isolation 7km (4 miles) north of Pafos. There's a small private beach on a picturesque bay.

✉ Kissonerga ☎ 2693 3900; www.cynthianahotel.com

POLIS-LAKKI AREA

Akamanthea Tourist Village (€)

A small, simple complex of studios and apartments with sea views. Self catering, but there are lots of facilities and a pool.

✉ Lakki, near Polis ☎ 2632 3500; www.akamanthea.com

Cyprotel Droushia Heights (€€)

Perched on an eyrie in the hills this hotel is away from everything; about 20 minutes to the nearest beach. Without a car a stay here will be exceedingly quiet. It is ideally situated for walks in the Akamas and the view over Chrysochou Bay is terrific.

✉ Drouseia, near Polis ☎ 2633 2351; www.dhcyprotels.com

Souli (€)

Comfortable, simply furnished rooms in a quiet hotel on the beach. There is an outdoor pool. The seafood restaurant is excellent.

✉ Lakki–Neo Chorio road ☎ 2632 1088

RESTAURANTS

PAFOS (PAPHOS)

Artio Brasserie (€€)

Expect light, international classics at this casual, stylish bistro, from big salads to melt-in-the-mouth beef *carpaccio*, along with delicious desserts.

✉ 6 Pyramou, off Tombs of the Kings Road, Pafos ☎ 2694 2800 🕐 Daily, dinner only

Cavallini (€€€)

A fount of tasteful modern Italian cuisine, with a stylishly rustic interior and an outside terrace that suffers from being a bit too close to a busy main street.

✉ 65 Leoforos Poseidonos, Kato Pafos ☎ 2696 4164 🕐 Daily 6:30–10:30

Deep Blue (€€)

A friendly restaurant with a modern nautical feel to it. Excellent seafood.

✉ 12 Odos Pafias Afroditis, Kato Pafos ☎ 2681 8015 🕐 Mon–Sat 6–11

Gina's Place (€€)
Casual bistro-café and wine bar serving gourmet sandwiches and salads with superior imported wines. Good delicatessen counter.

✉ 3 Odos Agiou Antoniou, Kato Pafos ☎ 2693 8017 🕔 Mon–Sat 9am–11pm (summer), 9–7 (winter)

Mandra Tavern (€€)
Revered by locals, this authentic taverna turns out excellent traditional Cypriot and Greek classics.

✉ 4 Dionysou, Kato Pafos ☎ 2693 4129 🕔 Daily, dinner only

Oriental Sushi Bar (€€)
When you've overdosed on *souvlaki*, head to this chic Japanese eatery for some of the best sushi in Cyrus.

✉ Elysium Hotel, Vasilissis Verenikis, Pafos ☎ 2684 4444 🕔 Daily, dinner only

Pelican (€–€€)
Few visitors can resist dining at Pafos's scenic harbour, but not many of the waterfront eateries meet their expectations. Pelican is a decent performer, but it is the setting people come for.

✉ 102 Leoforos Apostolou Pavlou, Kato Pafos ☎ 2694 6886 🕔 Daily

St George (€)
Serving up the freshest seafood on the west coast, this is the place to head for superb fried fish and chips.

✉ Agios Georgiou, near Pafos ☎ 2662 1306 🕔 Daily until 6pm

Seven St Georges (€€)
This award-winning restaurant serves gourmet Greek dishes with a twist, accompanied by the owner's own delicious earthy wines.

✉ Geroskipou, Pafos ☎ 2696 3176 🕔 Daily

POLIS-LAKKI AREA
Baths of Aphrodite (€)
Simple taverna serving good seafood, with spectacular views.

✉ Opposite Baths of Aphrodite trail start ☎ 2632 1457 🕔 Daily

Finikas (€)

Ideal for alfresco dining, with a varied menu.

✉ Polis Square ☎ 2632 3403 ⏰ Daily (Dec–Feb snacks only)

Moustakallis Tavern Restaurant (€€)

Family-run, with an excellent choice of Cypriot food.

✉ Off the south side of Polis Square ☎ 2632 2883 ⏰ Daily

Yiangos and Peter Taverna (€€)

See page 59.

SHOPPING

JEWELLERY

Athos Diamond Centre

Exclusive agents for many of the big names and *the* place to buy diamonds in Pafos.

✉ Shop 80 Leoforos Poseidonos, Kato Pafos ☎ 2681 1630

SOUVENIRS, HANDICRAFTS AND LEATHER

Costas Theodorou

Leather garments off the peg or made to measure.

✉ 92 Makarios Leoforos, Kato Pafos ☎ 2693 8390

Cyprus Handicraft Service

A wide selection of traditional Cypriot handicrafts made in Government-run workshops.

✉ 64 Leoforos Apostolou Pavlou, Kato Pafos ☎ 2630 6243

Fyti Village

The villagers produce fine woven cloth, especially pretty embroidered curtains and tablecloths.

Mosaics Plaza

Unique gifts and souvenirs in gold and silver, plus mineral and gemstone items. Also a section of leather goods.

✉ Harbour, Kato Pafos ☎ 2681 9999

STORES AND ARCADES
Debenhams
A very smart branch of this department store.
✉ Odos Lidras, Kato Pafos ☎ 2694 7122

ENTERTAINMENT AND SPORTS

CULTURAL EVENTS
Pafos Aphrodite Festival
Pafos Municipality organizes opera, theatre, music and dance events from the end of August to September at the medieval castle.
✉ Pafos ☎ 2682 2218

GOLF
Aphrodite Hills
This 18-hole course, set in the grounds of a 12th-century monastery in a valley, has several holes with views of the sea. Facilities include a restaurant, tennis and outdoor pool.
✉ Kouklia, north of Pafos ☎ 2682 8200

Secret Valley Golf Club
Not far from Kouklia, this 18-hole course is set in a scenic valley surrounded by rock formations.
✉ East of Pafos ☎ 2627 4000

Tsada Golf Club
✉ Tsada, 12km (7.5 miles) northeast of Pafos ☎ 2664 2774

HORSEBACK RIDING
George's Ranch
✉ Agios Georgios, near Peyia, 20km (12.5 miles) north of Pafos
☎ 2662 1064

TEN-PIN BOWLING
Cockatoos
✉ 25 Odos Agiou Antoniou, Kato Pafos ☎ 2682 2004 🕐 Daily 10–3

Nicosia and the High Troodos

Nicosia (Lefkosia) lies inland on the Mesaoria, or central plain. This location allowed the city to avoid the devastation wreaked on the coastal towns by Arab raiders. Here the plain is relatively narrow, with the Pentadaktylos Mountains to the north and the foothills of the Troodos approaching the city from the southwest.

Nicosia
(Lefkosia/Lefkoşa)

The northern boundary is no arbitrary choice: the Green Line that still divides Cyprus cuts through the heart of Nicosia. But visitors will now find it a frontier they can cross at the Ledra Palace Crossing in Nicosia, as well as at another couple of points in the area.

To the south is a splendid area of valleys and villages; Stavros tis Psokas in the west is a lonely forest station; Machairas Monastery and its surrounding hills make up the eastern extremity.

NICOSIA (LEFKOSIA)

Nicosia

Despite the opening of the border, Nicosia, the capital of Cyprus, remains a divided city. The border, known as the Green Line, separates the Greek Cypriot and Turkish Cypriot parts of the island and runs through the southern part of the city. The Greek Cypriot side has all the hallmarks of a modern westernized place and is a thriving shopping and business centre, though its ancient history is visible. The Turkish Cypriot sector has a more dilapidated look, with narrow, atmospheric streets and a bustling feel.

Nicosia is always busy and is hotter than the coast in the summer, so visitors should not plan too strenuous a programme. Fortunately the main attractions are within the old city walls and can be explored on foot.

An extensive modernization and refurbishment programme is under way in the old part of town, but progress is slow. The traffic-free Laiki Geitonia area is a pleasant place to wander, with all the facilities a tourist could need, and leads into some of the older shopping streets.

There is less to see in northern Nicosia but the narrow streets are fun to explore. However, almost all roads eventually lead to the main sight, the Selimiye Mosque, once the Cathedral of Santa Sophia, the minarets of which dominate this part of town. There are a number of other mosques in the vicinity, plus a few small museums and, for the more adventurous, the Turkish Baths.
✚ 16J

GREEK CYPRIOT NICOSIA

Agios Ioannis Cathedral

The cathedral lies within the grounds of the Byzantine Museum and was built in 1662 on the site of a Benedictine abbey church. It contains some fine 18th-century wall paintings and is ornately decorated throughout. It is claimed that it contained the finger of St John the Baptist until it was stolen by Mameluke raiders. The cathedral is smaller than one might expect of a building of importance and is best visited early.

✚ *Nicosia 3d* ✉ Plateia Archiepiskopou Kyprianou 🕒 Mon–Fri 8–12, 2–4, Sat 8–12 💶 Free 🍴 Cafés nearby (€)

Archbishop Makarios Cultural Centre, Byzantine Museum and Art Gallery

The most important exhibits in the museum are the 6th-century Kanakaria Mosaics, which were thought lost when they were stolen from their church on the Karpasia peninsula in northern Cyprus. They were recovered when offered for sale on the international art market and were returned to this purpose-built wing of the museum. On show are a large number of impressive icons from churches around the island.

✠ *Nicosia 3d* ✉ Plateia Archiepiskopou Kyprianou ☎ 2243 0008
🕐 Mon–Fri 9–4:30, Sat 9–1 ✋ Moderate 🍴 Cafés nearby (€)

Cyprus Museum

The museum houses most of the important finds from sites across Cyprus – neolithic artefacts, Bronze Age vases and clay figurines, Mycenaean objects from Kourion (➤ 42–43) and sophisticated pottery. Two thousand figurines found at Agia Irini are displayed as they were found, gathered around a single altar. A wide range of sculpture is on show, as well as a huge bronze statue of Roman Emperor Septimius Severus and the famous horned god from Enkomi. There are impressive items from Salamis (➤ 52–53), some mosaics and a reconstructed rock-cut tomb.

✠ *Nicosia 1d* ✉ Leoforos Mouseiou
☎ 2286 5888 🕐 Tue, Wed, Fri, Sat 9–5, Thu 8–4, Sun 10–1. Closed 1 Jan, 25 Dec, Greek Orthodox Easter Sun
✋ Moderate 🍴 Café opposite (€€)

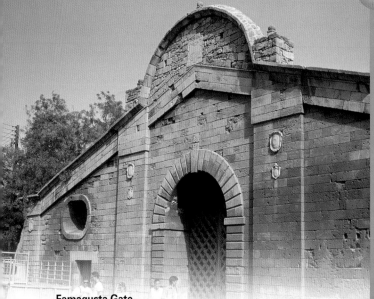

Famagusta Gate

This was the main entrance into the old city from the south and east. It is set into the historic walls and was restored to house a cultural centre used for exhibitions and other events, already this is currently closed for restoration.

✚ *Nicosia 4e* ✉ Leoforos Athinon 🍴 Cafés nearby (€)

Hadjigeorgakis Kornesios House
(Ethnographical Museum)

This house belonged to the grand dragoman of Cyprus, Hadjigeorgakis Kornesios, at the end of the 18th century. The dragoman was an interlocutor between the ethnic Greek and Turkish populations, an important and powerful role at that time. The museum contains a number of artefacts from the dragoman's life, displayed in reconstructions of some of the original rooms, along with letters and documents prepared by Kornesios.

✚ *Nicosia 3d* ✉ Odos Patriarchou Grigoriou ☎ 2230 5316 🕐 Tue, Wed, Fri, 8:30–3:30; Thu 8:30–5; Sat 9:30–3:30 👆 Inexpensive 🍴 Cafés nearby (€)

Laiki Geitonia

This is a revived traffic-free area of old Nicosia where traditional buildings have been restored. It is specifically aimed at the tourist, with a whole range of restaurants, craft shops, souvenir stores and the tourist office.The bustling shopping streets of Lidras and Onasagoras are not far from the Laiki Geitonia area and are also interesting places to wander. Look out for the odd traditional shop squeezed in between typical chain stores. At their northern end are the sandbags that mark the Green Line.

✚ *Nicosia 2d* ✉ Within old city walls, northeast of Plateia Eleftherias
🍴 Many cafés (€€)

Leventis Municipal Museum of Nicosia

This museum, in Laiki Geitonia, is well set out and modest in size. Medieval finds, some of which were uncovered when the building was being restored, are in the basement. The first floor deals with the period 2300BC to the Turkish era and the ground floor covers the British colonial time, as well as the city's recent history. The documentation from this later time is particularly interesting although the commentaries can be a little partisan.

✚ *Nicosia 2d* ✉ Odos Ippokratou ☎ 2266 1475 🕐 Tue–Sun 10–4:30.
Closed 1 Jan, 25 Dec, Greek Orthodox Easter Sun 👆 Free 🍴 Café in
basement (€€)

Omeriye Mosque

As with many of the city's mosques, this building was originally a church, converted in 1571 by Lala Mustafa Paşa, the occupying Turkish general. He believed that the visit of the Muslim prophet Omar should be commemorated, so the minaret was added and the old Lusignan tombstones used to cover the floor. The mosque is still used as a place of worship, so remove your shoes and women will need to wear a cloak borrowed from the mosque.

✚ *Nicosia 3d* ✉ Odos Trikoupi 🕐 Any reasonable hour but not during
prayer 👆 Free 🍴 Cafés nearby (€)

TURKISH CYPRIOT NICOSIA (LEFKOŞA)

Büyük Hamam

This was once the Church of St George, built in the 14th century and subsequently converted to a bathhouse by the Turks. The main room is domed, the floor well below street level. On Fridays only women are permitted inside, other days men only. Should it be* locked, the café owner on the west side has the key.

✚ *Nicosia 2e* ✉ Mousa Orfenbey Sokağı ◷ Jun–Sep daily 7:30–1, 4–6; Oct–May daily 8–1, 2–6 ✋ Free entry. Baths: moderate 🍴 Café next door (€)

Büyük Han

Built in 1572 by Lala Mustafa Paşa, the first Ottoman governor of Cyprus. It was a simple inn, complete with stables and a small mosque in the courtyard. Perhaps the nadir of its fortunes was when it became Nicosia's central prison in 1893. Its days of neglect are now over – the Department of Antiquities has restored it, and it now houses craft shops and cafés, as well as being a venue for concerts.

✚ *Nicosia 2e* ✉ Arasta Sokağı ◷ Mon, Wed–Thu, Sat 8–8, Tue and Fri 8pm–12

Lapidary Museum

The building, on two levels, was perhaps once the home of a wealthy Venetian family. Assorted wooden relics from mosques and churches display fine carving. In the courtyard is a random selection of Corinthian capitals, carved stone heads and a section of a beautiful rose window.

✚ *Nicosia 3e* ✉ Northeast of the Selimiye Mosque 🕐 Jun–Sep daily 9–2; Oct–May Tue–Sun 9–12:30, 1:30–5:45, Mon 3:30–5:45 ✋ Inexpensive

Mevlevi Tekke (Ethnographical Museum)

This was the home of the whirling dervishes, a sect founded in the 13th century. The rooms have a simple elegance, complete with a splendid minstrels' gallery looking down on where the dervishes, heads lowered in contemplation, would stretch out their arms and spin at ever increasing speed. In 1925 Kemal Atatürk forbade such dancing in an attempt to modernize Turkish culture. After 20 years the ruling was relaxed and the dance celebrated once more. To one side is a collection of costumes, wedding dresses and musical instruments.

✚ *Nicosia 2f* ✉ Girne Caddesi 🕐 Jun–Sep Mon–Fri 9–2; Oct–Mar daily 9–1, 2–4:45 ✋ Moderate

Selimiye Mosque

This impressive building was a Christian masterpiece before conversion to a mosque of the Ottoman Turks, the most important in Cyprus. The elevations of magnificent windows, portals and buttresses are discordant; the reason – the soaring minarets. They are landmarks in the walled city, and their imposition on the west front by the Turks reflects the momentous events of 1570–71.

The original cathedral was started in 1209 and substantially completed 117 years later. In reality it was never quite finished, work carrying on long after the consecration.

Everything changed with the arrival of the Turks. All the overt Christian decoration of the cathedral was destroyed. Soon work was started on the minarets and the building became the Cathedral of Santa Sophia until the name was changed to the Selimiye Mosque in 1954.

✚ *Nicosia 3e* ✉ Selimiye Sokağı 🕐 Daily ✋ Free

More to see in the High Troodos

AGIOS IRAKLEIDIOS

The monastery was founded in the Byzantine era, and it is dedicated to the saint who guided St Paul and St Barnabas to nearby Tamassos during their missionary travels. St Irakleidios lived in a cave, and the first church was built around it. His skull is kept in the present building in a silver reliquary, and many believe it has miraculous powers to heal the sick.

The complex is now a convent. It dates from 1773 and is a simple construction of good appearance, with excellent gardens. These are meticulously tended by the nuns and in summer are an oasis of greenery and colour in the barren landscape.

✚ 8E ✉ Near the village of Politikon ⏰ Group visits only: Mon, Tue, Thu 9–12 ✋ Free 🍴 Café opposite (€)

KAKOPETRIA

This village stands high in the poplar-lined Solea Valley and makes a great base for exploring the surrounding area. As hill villages go, it is quite large and is a popular weekend resort for Cypriots. It is certainly not a smart place, the buildings are generally old or ramshackle or both, but it has charm and many traditional dwellings are being restored. Kakopetria has a modern town where most of the restaurants, shops and hotels can be found. There is also a delightful ramshackle old quarter where two-storey stone houses are set along a cobblestoned pedestrian-only lane, and little alleys here and there are worth exploring.

Up the valley (3km/2 miles) is the church of **Agios Nikolaos tis Stegis** with its famous roof. Below the town, at Galata, are the tiny churches of Panagia Eleousa and Panagia Theotokos, looking like country barns, with their roofs nearly touching the ground.

✚ 6D

Agios Nikolaos tis Stegis

⏰ Tue–Sat 9–4, Sun 11–4 ✋ Free 🍴 Café (€)

MACHAIRAS MONASTERY

The monastery was founded in the 12th century and grew around an icon of the Virgin Mary. Successive fires destroyed the original church and its wall paintings and in 1892 the entire monastery was burned to the ground.

The present building dates from the early 20th century, and its elevations are fortress-like, broken up with wooden balconies. Within is an impressive iconostasis, illuminated by chandeliers. On feast days rituals take place starting early and culminating at midnight with the abbot emerging with the holy fire, a glowing candle. Its setting, overlooking a valley, is spectacular.

Outside, a track leads down the wooded valley to the cave of Grigoris Afxentiou, second in command of EOKA during the

uprising against the British. In 1957 a shepherd betrayed him and British soldiers surrounded the cave entrance. Afxentiou chose to fight, dying eight hours later in his hideout.

✚ 8D ✉ Near Fikardou, eastern Troodos ⏱ Visits only: Mon, Tue, Thu 9–12
✋ Free

MOUNT OLYMPOS

At 1,951m (6,401ft) above sea level, the summit of Mount Olympos is the highest ground in Cyprus. It is not an inaccessible peak, as a narrow road winds towards the top, stopping just below the summit at an unappealing radar dome and other military facilities. As a mountain it is thereby compromised, with no chance of proceeding higher to experience the view. This is reserved for

those on the other, more inaccessible, side of the hill. In winter it is an unforgettable experience to stand in deep snow, bathed in sunlight, and look over to Morfou Bay and the Taurus Mountains of Turkey beyond.

✚ 5D ✉ 55km (34 miles) from Limassol, 97km (60 miles) from Nicosia
🍽 Cafés in Troodos village 4km (2.5 miles) away (€)

PANAGIA TOU ARAKA

The paintings in this church are marvellous. Unfortunately the drive to get there is long and tiring, albeit through superb scenery. Should the church be locked, admission is then by courtesy of the priest, normally found in the village of Lagoudera.

The church retains the most complete series of wall paintings of the Byzantine period on the island and they have been restored, courtesy of UNESCO. They represent the metropolitan classicizing school in full bloom. Even visitors who know little of this Byzantine style will surely appreciate their magnificence.

✚ 7D ✉ Lagoudera 🕐 Daily 10–4 🎟 Free 🍽 Café in nearby village (€)

a drive into the Troodos Mountains

For Pafos visitors, the drive proper starts 17km (10.5 miles) towards Limassol. On the motorway, take the Mandria exit

Turn left at the Xeros River for Nikokleia, Mamonia and Agios Georgios. It is a splendid 55km (34 miles) up to Platres (Pano), through orchards and farmland.

The route from Limassol begins about 13km (8 miles) to the west, immediately after Erimi. Motorway drivers should use the Kantou exit.

Take the road north to Kantou, Souni and Agios Amvrosios. About 37km (23 miles) of pleasant uphill driving leads to Omodos village, now a popular tourist attraction. It is another 14km (8.5 miles) to meet up with the Pafos travellers at Platres.

Traverse the confusing streets of Platres to reach the Nicosia–Limassol highway and go left up to Troodos village – about 7km (4 miles). The route runs for 11km (7 miles) along the minor road to Prodromos, the highest village in Cyprus.

Soon after Prodromos the descent becomes dramatic, as the road twists and turns above the abyss.

This is a cherry-growing area, and its main villages – Pedoulas, Moutoullas and Kalopanagiotis – are reached in succession. Moutoullas is also famous for its spring water. After the excitement of the hairpin bends, it is a

simple run of about 8km (5 miles) before sweeping east towards Linou and the Limassol–Nicosia highway.

Turn right for Troodos/Limassol and climb the mountain. Kakopetria (▶ 152), after 14km (8.5 miles), is worth the detour. At Troodos village, Limassol-bound drivers continue for 55km (34 miles), via Trimiklini and Pano Polemedia. For Pafos turn off at Platres to reverse the route via Mandria, Agios Nikolaos and Mamonia.

Distance Limassol – 200km (124 miles); Pafos – 220km (136 miles)
Time 5–8 hours
Start/end point Limassol or Pafos ✚ 7B or 2C
Lunch Tavernas Platres ✉ Pedoulas

PANAGIA TOU ASINOU

The fame of this church is such that it is quite a surprise to find it so tiny, hidden on a hillside of eucalyptus and pine trees. A steep clay-tiled outer roof protects the vulnerable Byzantine dome and treasures within. The frescoes are the best of Cyprus's painted churches, the earliest dating back to the 12th century. They were added to over the years and culminate in the powerful work by refugee painters from Asia Minor.

Christ is depicted in the sanctuary and the dome of the narthex, gazing down. All around, the rank and file are beautifully illustrated.

✚ 6E ✉ Nikitari ⏱ Summer daily 9–5; winter 9:30–1, 2–4; ask in Nikitari for the priest with the key ✋ Free

PANAGIA TOU KIKKOU

Best places to see, ➤ 50–51.

HOTELS

GREEK CYPRIOT NICOSIA (LEFKOSIA)

Averof (€)

Traditional hotel in a quiet area just outside the city.

✉ 19 Odos Averof ☎ 2277 3447; www.averof.com.cy

Centrum (€€)

The large rooms may not live up to the promise of the stylish lobby area, but they are clean and comfortable and the location – in the heart of the old-town action – can't be beaten.

✉ 15 Odos Pasikratous, Eleftherias Square ☎ 2245 6444; www.centrumhotel.net

Cleopatra (€€)

Unfortunately the drab rooms don't live up to expectations formed from the stylish public spaces, but the pool is a luxury in Nicosia and the bar and the restaurant are popular.

✉ 8 Odos Florinis ☎ 2284 4000; www.cleopatra.com.cy

Hilton Cyprus (€€€)

See page 76.

TURKISH CYPRIOT NICOSIA (LEFKOŞA)

City Royal (€)

Modern hotel with extensive facilities and indoor pool.

✉ 19 Kemal Asik Caddesi ☎ 228 7611; www.city-royal.com

Saray (€€)

Central location and high standards make this a popular choice.

✉ Atatürk Meydanı ☎ 228 3115

AGROS

Rodon (€€)

This big traditionally built stone hotel in the Valley of the Roses has mountain views. There is an outdoor pool and a good restaurant.

✉ 1 Odos Rodou ☎ 2551 1201; www.rodonhotel.com

KAKOPETRIA
Linos Inn (€€)
The inn occupies several restored old houses in the conservation area. Character exudes from wooden beams, four-poster beds and antiques. However, the rooms have modern facilities – whirlpool baths, satellite television and heating in winter.

✉ Odos Palaias 34 ☎ 2292 3161

The Mill Hotel (€€)
See pages 77.

PEDOULAS
Mountain Rose (€)
Cosy hotel with balconies and splendid village and mountain views.

✉ Pedoulas ☎ 2295 2727

PLATRES
Kallithea Hotel (€€)
Set among pine trees in this lovely mountain village, handy for Mount Olympos.

✉ 89 Panagias Faneromenis ☎ 2542 1746

RESTAURANTS

GREEK CYPRIOT NICOSIA (LEFKOSIA)
Abu Faysal (€€)
Sophisticated Lebanese cuisine served in an elegant villa setting.

✉ 31 Odos Klimentou ☎ 2276 0353 ◷ Tue–Sun

Bistrot 1900 (€€)
Warm French bistro atmosphere, interesting starters and fine steaks only let down by the occasional misfire from the kitchen.

✉ Plateia Eleftherias ☎ 2266 7668 ◷ Daily

Erodos (€€)
In the old city by the Omeriye mosque, this is a reminder of an older Cyprus. There is Cypriot food and occasional Greek music.

✉ 11 Odos Patriarchou Grigoriou ☎ 2275 2250 ◷ Daily

Plaka (€€)

Situated among traditional houses in the new part of town, the speciality here is a seemingly never-ending meal of *meze*.

✉ 8 Stylianos Lenas ☎ 2276 5501 🕐 Daily, dinner only

Sitio (€€)

Watch the world go by from this café/restaurant. International dishes with a Mediterranean touch.

✉ 43 Leoforos Archiepiskopou Makariou III (at Odos Iras) ☎ 2245 8610 🕐 Daily

Xefoto (€€)

This Laiki Geitonia café-restaurant sets itself apart from the run of traditional eateries in the area with excellent Cypriot and Mediterranean food and live music.

✉ 6 Odos Aeschylou ☎ 2266 6567 🕐 Daily

Zanettos (€)

This hidden gem (with two sprawling dining rooms tucked away out back) is a perennial local favourite. The set-price menu includes myriad plates of *meze* and meat dishes. Booking essential.

✉ 65 Trikoupi ☎ 2276 5501 🕐 Daily, dinner only

TURKISH CYPRIOT NICOSIA (LEFKOŞA)

Boghijalian (€€)

A restaurant much frequented by the locals, who enjoy a cuisine that embraces the best Turkish dishes.

✉ Arapahemet ☎ 228 0700 🕐 Daily

Califorian Restaurant (€€)

The chef is a master of grilled meat dishes.

✉ Dereböyu ☎ 227 6938 🕐 Daily

El Sabor Latino (€€)

Stylish restaurant serving Spanish and Italian dishes. One of Nicosia's 'in' places. with live piano music on Saturday nights.

✉ 29 Selimiye Meydanı ☎ 228 8322 🕐 Daily

Kibris Ashevi (Cyprus Kitchen) (€)

Interior design includes traditional fixtures and fittings. The delicious pot roast from the clay oven must be ordered in advance.

✉ 39A Atatürk Caddesi ☎ 223 1751 ⏰ Daily

Saricizmeli (€)

One of the best-value restaurants in the capital. Select hearty traditional dishes from a buffet.

✉ 174 Girne Caddesi ☎ 227 3782 ⏰ Daily

Zir Locanta (€)

Small restaurant that serves consistently good local dishes.

✉ Istanbul Caddesi ☎ 714 3064 ⏰ Daily, dinner only

KAKOPETRIA
Linos Inn (€€)

In the historic area, this restaurant in the Linos hotel is rural in style with good traditional dishes.

✉ 34 Odos Palaias ☎ 2292 3161 ⏰ Daily

PLATRES
To Anoi (€€)

Family taverna serving local fare and with valley views.

✉ Platres centre ☎ 2542 2900 ⏰ Daily

Yiolandel (€€)

The paint may be fading a little but the Sunday buffet is excellent and the homemade cakes are delicious.

✉ 3B Leoforos Makariou, near Pendeli Hotel ☎ 2542 1720 ⏰ Daily

SHOPPING

JEWELLERY
Metaxas Jewellers

Beautiful gold, silver and diamond jewellery, the best evoking classical Cypriot pieces.

⏰ 205 Ledra, Nicosia ☎ 2266 6486 ⏰ Daily 9–1

Stephanides and Sons Jewellers

Long-established; superb designs inspired by antiquities.

🌐 23 Leoforos Archiepiskopou Makariou III, Nicosia ☎ 2266 1776

SOUVENIRS, HANDICRAFTS AND LEATHER

Cyprus Corner

This old-fashioned store is crammed with interesting antiques and old bric-a-brac, from goats' bells to wooden bread bowls.

🌐 Old Centre, Lefkosa (Turkish Cypriot Nicosia) ☎ 227 9347

Cyprus Handicraft Centre

This centre, along with those in other towns, promotes and sells Cypriot handicrafts.

✉ 186 Leoforos Athalassis, Nicosia ☎ 2230 5024

Laiki Geitonia

Refurbished, traffic-free tourist area of the walled city; craft shops.

✉ East of Plateia Eleftherias, Nicosia (walled city)

Leventis Museum Gift Shop

Reproductions of historical artefacts, including some jewellery.

✉ 17 Odos Ippokratous, Nicosia (walled city) ☎ 2267 1997

Nicos Michalias Studio

High-quality, hand-painted ceramic tiles, plates, street numbers and coasters in traditional designs.

✉ 33 Odos Lefkonos, Nicosia (walled city) ☎ 2275 3400

STORES AND ARCADES

Arasta Sokağı, Nicosia

Small shops, good for fabrics and inexpensive jeans and jackets.

Capital Center, Nicosia

The first real shopping centre in Cyprus is still worth a look.

✉ Leoforos Archiepiskopou Makariou III, Nicosia

City Plaza
Good multi-level department store.

✉ Leoforos Archiepiskopou Makariou III, Nicosia

Debenhams
This swanky branch of Debenhams is more chic than most.

✉ Leoforos Archiepiskopou Makariou III, Nicosia ☎ 2284 9000

Mehmet Akif Caddesi, Nicosia
Head for the centre of this long street to browse upmarket boutiques. Plenty of cheap and cheerful outlets are here too.

ENTERTAINMENT AND SPORT

CULTURAL EVENTS
Artos Foundation
This former bakery has been splendidly restored into an arts and cultural centre hosting exhibitions, performances, screenings and seminars.

✉ 64 Odos Agios Omologites, Nicosia ☎ 2244 5455; www.artosfoundation.org

Rembetika
A night out enjoying some traditional *rembetika* (Greek blues-style folk music) is a must and Mouskiki Tavern is the best place.

✉ Agiou Ilarionos, Nicosia ☎ 2234 9643 🕓 Fri, Sat night

HORSEBACK RIDING
Nicosia Riding Club
Riding on summer days in Troodos Square on Mount Olympos.

✉ Lythrodontas, 15km (9 miles) south of Nicosia ☎ 9967 1789

SKIING
Mount Olympos
Season is January to March. Hire ski equipment in Sun Valley.

Cyprus Ski Club
✉ Mount Olympos ☎ 2267 5340; www.cyprusski.com

The North

Famagusta
(Ammochostos/
Gazimağusa)

This is the Turkish-controlled part of Cyprus, underpopulated compared to the remainder of the island. Change has been slow in coming, perhaps

due to the easy-going temperament of the Turkish Cypriots, but since the opening of the border in 2003 the pace has been steadily picking up.

Whatever the objectives of trade embargoes on this area, they cannot detract from the magnificent scenery, and they have, to a diminishing extent, held back destructive mass tourism.

Along the north shore the spectacular Pentadaktylos (Beşparmak) Mountains run unbroken for 90km (56 miles). To the south the land is flat, opening out into the Mesaoria east of Nicosia. In summer it is impressively barren: in spring the colour has to be seen to be believed.

The narrow Karpasia peninsula is spectacular, with the blue Mediterranean visible to north and south.

FAMAGUSTA (GAZIMAĞUSA)

The city is divided, although not between Greek Cypriot and
Turkish Cypriot. Varosha, the new town, with its painted hotels
bordering the sandy beach, is closed to all but the military, as it
has been since 1974. Visitors concentrate on the walled city. They
are adequately compensated in that it is one of the finest
surviving examples of medieval military architecture.

To pass through the massive walls is to pass through history,
from the time of the Lusignans, Genoese and Venetians to the
bloody siege by the Turks in 1570–71. They stormed the walls
and all Cyprus was theirs for over 300 years.

In the narrow streets some shops remain unchanged by time
or fashion. Dark interiors hide a miscellany of goods. The town
can be a bustling place of noise and activity, but more often it is
calm. They may not be as outgoing as their Greek Cypriot
countrymen in the south, but Turkish Cypriots are equally
courteous and helpful.

There is much unexpected open space in all directions: an
attractive panorama of gardens where palm trees shade ancient
domed churches. Crumbling medieval buildings are all around.
The battered minaret and massive buttress of Lala Mustafa Paşa
Mosque form an impressive landmark.

✠ 21H

Lala Mustafa Paşa Mosque

The building has been a mosque for over 400 years, but the
architecture is of a Gothic cathedral. There is a single minaret,
well executed but certainly out of place. Even so, you can still
admire the splendid six-light window of the west front. Three
portals lead to the impressive interior, where Moslem simplicity
has allowed the fine nave to survive the loss of its Christian
decoration.

Lala Mustafa was the victorious commander of the Ottoman
Turks when they broke into Famagusta in 1571. Surprisingly, the

mosque only received his name in 1954, before which it was called the Mosque of Santa Sophia.

✉ Naim Efendi Sokağı 🕐 Daily 🎟 Free 🍴 Cafés all around (€)

St George of the Greeks

This is a substantial church, though it has deteriorated significantly (it was built in 1359). A dome covered the middle section of the church, but it collapsed under cannon fire in 1571. Some wall paintings survive, the best being in the eastern apse.

✉ Mustafa Ersu Sokağı 🕐 Daily 🎟 Free

a walk around Famagusta (Gazimağusa)

The walk starts at the Land Gate entrance of the historic walled city.

Istiklal Caddesi is directly opposite and should be followed, taking care not to lose it at the three-way junction after 130m (140yds).

About 130m (140yds) farther, on the left, is the church of St Peter and St Paul (▶ 170).

A right turn along Sinan Paşa Sokağı leads to the Palazzo del Provveditore (Venetian Palace).

From here it is a short distance to Namık Kemal Meydanı, overlooked by the magnificent west front of Lala Mustafa Paşa Mosque (▶ 166–167).

A short retreat (to the west) picks up Kısla Sokağı, and in 130m (140yds) are the twin churches (now restored) of the Knights Templar and Knights Hospitaller. Immediately beyond the churches the road turns right, to the northeast, and in 120m (130yds) Cafer Paşa Sokagı.

At the eastern end are the ruined, but impressive buttresses and lancet windows of St George of the Latins. The Citadel (Othello's Tower), a short distance to the north, should not be missed.

The walk continues alongside the sea wall, down Canbulat Yolu, to reach the splendid Sea Gate after 200m (220yds).

In another 160m (175yds), a short detour along Mustafa Ersu Sokağı brings you to the substantial church of St George of the Greeks (➤ 167). Returning to the main road, the Canbulat Museum is reached in 300m (330yds).

The return to the Land Gate is about 1,100m (just over half a mile). Pass outside the walls at the Canbulat Museum and follow the south wall.

Distance 2.75km (1.7 miles)
Time 1–3.5 hours
Start/end point Land Gate
Lunch Cafés in square around Lala Mustafa Paşa Mosque (€)

St Peter and St Paul (Sinan Paşa Mosque)

This Gothic church is distinctive for its spectacular flying buttresses. It was subsequently used as a mosque, as the ruined minaret in one corner testifies, and has also served as the municipal library. At other times it stored potatoes and grain and was known as the wheat mosque. On entering, the reason for the massive buttresses is apparent – the nave is of tremendous height, exerting a colossal force on the outside walls.

✉ Abdullah Paşa Sokağı 🕓 Jun–Sep Mon–Fri 9–2; Oct–May Mon–Fri 9–1, 2–4:45 👋 Inexpensive 🍴 Cafés nearby (€)

Venetial Walls

The original plan of the town was laid out by the Lusignans, but when the Venetians took over in 1489 they completely renovated the enclosing walls. Experts in military architecture, they lowered the walls but increased the thickness, taking out all features that were vulnerable to cannon fire.

Any tour of the fortifications should take into account the great heat of summer and the low parapets everywhere.

The Citadel should be visited. It is also known as Othello's Tower, a name derived from Shakespeare's play, set in 'Cyprus. A seaport' and 'Cyprus. The Citadel'. Four great cylindrical towers guard the corners of the Citadel, and the carving over the entrance is an impressive winged lion of St Mark. The great hall is a massive vaulted chamber.

Taking a clockwise circuit of the walls, the Sea Gate, 200m (220yds) southeast, is the next place of interest. The gate's portcullis is part of the original Venetian work. In another 500m (545yds) is the Canbulat Gate and bastion (Canbulat was a Turkish hero of the siege), now a museum. Muskets and swords are displayed next to period dresses finished with fine embroidery.

Three bastions on the south wall lead to the Land Gate, the main entrance to the town. It is part of the Ravelin, a bastion considered impregnable when built, but later found wanting as its ditch offered cover to the enemy.

🕐 Citadel and Museum: Jun–Sep daily 9–7; Oct–May 9–1, 2–4:45 💰 Citadel: moderate. Museum: inexpensive 🍴 Cafés nearby (€)

More to see in the North

AGIOS ILARION CASTLE

Best places to see,
➤ 36–37.

BELAPAIS ABBEY

The setting of the abbey on the northern slopes of the Pentadaktylos (Beşparmak) Mountains is marvellous. Far below are almond and olive groves on the coastal plain, and Keryneia (Girne) seen to the west. Augustinian canons founded the abbey at the end of the 12th century, its importance lasting for some 300 years. The cloister is half ruined and flamboyant tracery hangs down from the pointed arches. On the north side is the refectory, where the vault appears to spring from the supporting capitals. Six tall windows look out on to the northern shore, and there is an exquisite pulpit, reached by stairs constructed in the thickness of the wall.

In 1995 forest fires swept through the Pentadaktylos Mountains, advancing rapidly on Belapais (Beylerbeyi), the village where the author Lawrence Durrell lived from 1953 to 1956. In his celebrated *Bitter Lemons* he had written 'two things spread quickly; gossip and a forest fire'. It was only good fortune and the skill of the firefighters that prevented the destruction of Belapais.

🖬 16K 🖂 Belapais (Beylerbeyi) village 🕒 Jun–Sep daily 9–7; Oct–May daily 9–4:45 📷 Moderate 🍴 Cafés nearby (€)

KANTARA

Kantara is the most easterly of the great Lusignan fortresses of the northern shore. At 600m (1,968ft) above sea level, its walls crown rocky crags, with the north shore way below.

The location at the eastern end of the Pentadaktylos (Beşparmak) Mountains gave the garrison control of the Karpasia peninsula. Visitors can, in a brief panorama, survey this unique landscape in its entirety.

Most of the castle is a ruin, although the formidable outer wall is substantially intact. Entrance is gained through a ruined barbican and two towers. Steps lead on to vaulted chambers and medieval latrines. On the highest ground, only a Gothic window remains.

✚ 21L ✉ Near Kantara village ◉ Jun–Sep daily 10–5; Oct–May daily 9–1, 2–4:45 ✋ Moderate 🍴 Cafés in Kantara village (€)

KERYNEIA (GIRNE)

Keryneia is unmatched in the rest of Cyprus. This is all to do with the harbour and its magnificent setting. Certainly the old buildings of the quayside, with the exception of the customs houses, have all been reconstituted as restaurants and bars, nevertheless everything seems just perfect, day or night.

A huge cylindrical bastion from Venetian times forms the east end of the harbour, a minaret rises up in the middle ground and the bell-tower of the former Archangelos Michaïl church, now an icon museum, is in the west. Mountain ridges and summits run unbroken into the hazy distance.

The origins of the **castle** are Lusignan, but it was the Venetians who made it impregnable (and then surrendered it to the Turks without a fight in 1570). Inside, sunlight streams down from hidden windows and openings. Entry into the complex structure is over the moat, now dry, to reach a gatehouse. Progress is then up a ramp, passing a small Byzantine chapel and continuing to the northwest tower, where there is the tomb of Sadık Paşa, killed in 1570. Various routes can be taken to complete a tour of the castle, but care is needed to keep clear of the unguarded drops.

The Shipwreck Museum within the castle is a highlight. It houses the remains of a Hellenistic-era merchant ship, raised from the seabed between 1968 and 1969. The blackened hull, astonishingly well preserved, is more than 2,300 years old.

🚌 16K 🍴 Cafés around the harbour (€–€€)

Keryneia Castle

✉ Harbour 🕐 Jun–Sep daily 9–8; Oct–May daily 9–4:45
✋ Expensive

SALAMIS

Best places to see, ➤ 52–53.

SOLOI (SOLI)

The founders of Soli came from Greece and they created a city destined to play a major role in the struggle against Persian rule in the 5th and 4th centuries BC. However, only the later work of the Romans survives. They cut a theatre out of a rocky hillside overlooking Morfou Bay; today, most of this substantial work is a reconstruction. The remains of a colonnade leading to an agora are under a massive awning. Some mosaics remain, the bird representations being most impressive.

The wealth of Soli lay with its copper, mined from the surrounding hills. Boats from the city's harbour, long silted up, carried the metal to various parts of the Mediterranean.

✚ 5F ✉ Near Gemikonağı
☎ 727 8035 ⏰ Jun–Sep daily 9–7; Oct–May daily 9–4:45
✋ Expensive

VOUNI

The road to ruined Vouni Palace spirals spectacularly around a mountain, the sea on one side and the Troodos Mountains on the other. A series of terraces, swept bare by time, climb the hillside. The palace was clearly a substantial construction, with apartments, baths and courtyards. It was built in the 5th century BC by a pro-Persian king from Marion, possibly to counter the power of nearby Soli, a city loyal to the Greeks. The baths have a water system comparable to those of the Romans, but it is centuries earlier. At the top of the hill are the ruins of the Greek-style Temple of Athena.

➕ 5F ✉ Near Gemikonağı 🕐 Jun–Sep daily 10–5; Oct–May daily 9–1, 2–4:45 ✋ Expensive

HOTELS

BELAPAIS (BEYLERBEYI) AREA

Ambelia Village (€€)
An apartment complex that stands high above the village of Belapais (Beylerbeyi).

✉ Belapais–Kato Dhikomo road ☎ 815 3655

Bellapais Gardens (€€)
See page 76.

FAMAGUSTA (GAZIMAĞUSA) AREA

Delcraft (€€)
Experience an authentic working village at Cyprus' first eco-village. Stay in simple rooms in a traditional stone house.

✉ Büyükkonuk village, Karpaz Peninsula ☎ 383 2038; www.ecotourismcyprus.com

Karpaz Arch Houses (€€)
See page 77.

Mimoza (€)
This peppermint-painted hotel is located at the water's edge on a sandy beach, near ancient Salamis.

✉ Just north of Salamis ☎ 378 8219

Palm Beach (€€€)
Comfortable hotel on the seafront with a casino and pool among its entertainments.

✉ Leoforos Havva Sentürk, Deve Limani ☎ 366 2000; www.northernpalmbeach.com

Portofino (€)
Basic family-run hotel near the old town.

✉ 9 Fevzi Çakmak Bulvarı ☎ 366 4392; www.portofinohotel-cyprus.com

Salamis Bay Conti Resort (€€€)
See page 77.

KERYNEIA (GIRNE) AND THE WEST

Altinkaya Resort (€)

A family-run place with 42 single-storey buildings near a swimming pool. The on-site restaurant is popular.

✉ Kazafani (Ozanköy) ☎ 815 5001; www.altinkaya-cyprus.com

Bristol (€)

Good value accommodation with access to parking.

✉ 114 Ziya Rizki Caddesi ☎ 815 6556

British (€)

Good Keryneia harbour location. There are great views from the restaurant and roof terrace.

✉ Eftal Afca Caddesi, Kordonboyu, west end of harbour, Keryneia
☎ 815 2240; www.britishhotelcyprus.com

Dome (€€)

The longest established hotel in Cyprus occupies a prime position on a rocky outcrop near the harbour. A seawater swimming pool is built into a rocky enclosure to the front of the hotel.

✉ Kordonboyu Caddesi, Keryneia ☎ 815 2453

Dorana (€)

Within an easy walk of the shopping area and harbour with stylish renovated rooms.

✉ 143 Ziya Rizki Caddesi, west of the harbour, Keryneia ☎ 815 3521

Lefke Gardens (€)

Minutes from the sea, on Güzelyurt Bay, this traditional hotel has lots of charm.

✉ Lefke, Güzelyurt ☎ 728 8223

Nostalgia Hotel (€)

In a restored old building with traditionally decorated rooms and centrally located, this budget hotel is great value.

✉ 22 Cafer Pasa Sokak, Keryneia ☎ 815 3079

Rocks Hotel and Casino (€€€)

This elegant luxury hotel has beautifully appointed rooms with all mod cons.

✉ 102 Kordonboyu Caddesi, Keryneia ☎ 815 2379; www.rockshotel.com

RESTAURANTS

FAMAGUSTA (GAZIMAĞUSA) AREA

Akdeniz (€)

Lively and popular with the locals, this roadside restaurant has a wide, shady terrace. The seafood is delicious.

✉ Just north of Salamis Bay Hotel ☎ 378 8227 🕔 Daily

Cyprus House (€€)

This old village house is decorated in 1930s style. Don't miss the mouth-watering local delicacies. Advisable to book.

✉ Polat Paşa Bulvarı, Famagusta, opposite post office ☎ 366 4845 🕔 Lunch and dinner; closed Sun

KERYNEIA (GIRNE) AND SURROUNDING AREA

The Address (€€)

Stunning situation, right by the sea; book a table on the terrace and feast on succulent kebabs and other Turkish-Cypriot dishes.

✉ 13 Ali Aktas Sokak, Karaoğlanoğlu ☎ 822 3537 🕔 Daily

Altınkaya 1 (€€)

Popular with locals, its sits atop the cliffs overlooking a scenic stretch of coastline. Renowned for its fish dishes.

✉ Alsancak, 8km (5 miles) west of Keryneia ☎ 821 8341 🕔 Thu–Tue

Altınkaya 2 (€€)

A rich variety of seafood, plus Turkish and English dishes.

✉ Osanköy, towards Belapais (Beylerbeyi) ☎ 815 5001 🕔 Lunch and dinner

The Ambiance (€€)

A la carte cuisine or 'full kebab' in a stunning seashore setting.

✉ Signposted off the main Keryneia (Girne)–Lapithos (Lapta) road at Karaoğlanoğlu ☎ 822 2849 🕔 Daily

Bellapais Gardens Restaurant (€€)

A delightful room, refined cooking of very fresh ingredients and charismatic service. Their local specialties (kebabs and lamb chops) could be the best you'll try on your trip.

✉ Crusader Road, Belapais (Beylerbeyi) ☎ 815 6066; www.bellapaisgardens.com ✪ Daily

Café Dükkan (€)

Popular with locals as much as British expats, this arty café has friendly service and a menu that includes European café standards (toasted sandwiches and salads), alongside Cypriot dishes.

✉ Mete Adanir Caddesi, Keryneia ☎ 815 2200 ✪ Daily

Cenap (€€)

With its live music, and guests and staff who break out in 'spontaneous' dancing on a fairly regular basis, this makes for a fun night out. Expect traditional Cypriot cuisine and an excellent 'full kebab'.

✉ 27 Ankara Caddesi, Keryneia ☎ 821 8417 ✪ Daily

The Courtyard Inn (€€)

This popular restaurant, with its country pub atmosphere, is run by expatriates from the UK. Also open for bar snacks, and the roast on Sunday is good value.

✉ Karakum village, about 2km (1 mile) east of Keryneia ☎ 815 5566 ✪ Daily

The Crows Nest (€€)

Pub and restaurant that caters for visitors and the villagers. Cosy atmosphere and open-plan kitchen. The menu embraces Turkish and continental cuisine.

✉ Karaman village ☎ 822 2567 ✪ Daily

Efendi (€€)

This stylish restaurant, tucked away in Keryneia's back streets, is popular and a reservation is advisable if you'd like to sample the fusion cuisine.

✉ 6 Kamil Paşa Sokak Caddesi, Keryneia ☎ 815 1149 ✪ Tue–Sat 6pm–late

Guler's Fish Restaurant (€€)

Well sited overlooking a cove by the shore. Many of the locals claim that the best fish in Keryneia is served here.

✉ Keryneia, to the west by the Serif Hotel Apartments ☎ 822 2718 🕐 Daily

Harbour Club (€€€)

French cuisine, first-class seafood and many typical Turkish dishes with a splendid view over the harbour.

✉ Harbour (near castle), Keryneia ☎ 815 2211 🕐 Daily

The Hideaway Club (€€)

International dishes in a poolside restaurant with mountain views.

✉ Trimithi–Karmi road, Karaman ☎ 822 2620 🕐 Daily

Hilarion Village Restaurant (€€)

Tasty local dishes on the rarefied heights of the Keryneia hills.

✉ Karmi ☎ 822 2574 🕐 Daily

Jashan (€€€)

Excellent Indian cuisine and friendly service. Booking is advisable during the high season.

✉ Keryneia (Girne)–Lapithos (Lapta) road, Karaoğlanoğlu 🕐 Daily

Lagoon Seafood Restaurant (€€)

Choose your freshly caught fish from the display case, then have one of the most refined seafood meals you'll have in Keryneia.

✉ Kordonboyu Caddesi, Keryneia ☎ 815 2160 🕐 Daily

Laughing Buddha (€€)

The finest and most authentic Chinese on the northern side of the island, this attractive restaurant is justifiably popular.

✉ Ecevit Caddesi, Keryneia ☎ 815 8715 🕐 Daily

Lemon Tree (€€)

Excellent Turkish Cypriot menu including hot stuffed pastries, grilled fish and meat plus good *meze*. Long-established.

✉ Çatalköy road, 5km (3 miles) east of Keryneia ☎ 824 4045 🕐 Daily

Mirage (€€)
This stylish eatery-café-bar serves up Turkish-Cypriot dishes alongside classic international bistro food.
✉ Gonyeli Caddesi, Keryneia ☎ 223 2730 🕓 Daily

Missina (€€)
While the seafood here is superb, the main reason to reserve a table is the waterfront location, within a splash from the sea.
✉ Omer Faydali Sokok, Karaoğlanoğlu ☎ 822 3844 🕓 Daily

Mountain House (€€)
European and Turkish cuisine in an established family concern.
✉ Belapais (Beylerbeyi) road, Keryneia ☎ 815 3881 🕓 Mon–Sat lunch only; closed Sun

Niazi's (€)
This popular restaurant is considered by many to be Keryneia's best. The cooking of kebabs has been turned into an art form – go for the 'full kebab'.
✉ West of the harbour, opposite Dome Hotel, Keryneia ☎ 815 2160 🕓 Daily

The Old Mill (€)
Simple but tasty fare served in an eclectically decorated old olive mill.
✉ Central Ozanköy ☎ 815 6818 🕓 Thu–Tue dinner only

Rafters Pub and Bistro (€€)
Snack and bistro menu to suit all appetites. Special requests cooked to order but notice required. Booking advisable.
✉ Ozanköy road, 4km (2.5 miles) east of Keryneia ☎ 815 2946 🕓 Tue–Sat 6–12, Sun 12–7

Tree of Idleness (€€)
Fish and kebab dishes and Turkish Cypriot *meze*. Live music Saturday. Courtesy shuttle to hotels in Keryneia. Some dispute the claim to host Durrell's famous tree, but it doesn't dampen the

enthusiasm of the many who pile in for Saturday 'Cyprus nights'.
✉ Belapais (Beylerbeyi) ☎ 815 3380 🕐 Daily

Trypiti (€€)
See page 59.

Valley View Restaurant (€€)
The menu is impressive – daily fresh fish and seafood, full kebab, chicken dishes, *meze* and others.
✉ Yani, Çatalköy ☎ 868 7070 🕐 Daily

The Veranda (€€)
Seaside restaurant with a varied menu. Booking advisable.
✉ Sehit Ridvan Caddesi, eastern end of Karaoğlanoğlu ☎ 822 2053
🕐 Tue–Sun

MORFOU (GÜZELYURT) AREA
CMC Fish and Chips (€)
With a simple menu, this restaurant claims to be the best for traditional British-style fish and chips in Cyprus.
✉ Ydidalga ☎ 727 7439 🕐 Daily

Iskele (€€)
Seafood and vegetable *meze*. Live music at the weekends.
✉ Güzelyurt town centre ☎ 714 2099 🕐 Daily

Şah Restaurant (€€)
Kebab and excellent Turkish *meze*. Live music some nights.
✉ Güzelyurt, next to roundabout at entrance to town, arriving from north coast ☎ 714 3064 🕐 Daily

SHOPPING
SOUVENIRS, HANDICRAFTS AND LEATHER
Ceramic Centre
Largest pottery showroom in the North.
✉ Ortaköy, 3km (2 miles) northwest of Nicosia ☎ 223 2302

Fanus

This store stocks splendid souvenirs and handicrafts, from ceramic bowls, plates and tiles to colourful Oriental lamps.

✉ Canbulat Sokak, Keryneia ☎ 846 6964

Gordes

Cyprus' best carpet shop has a wide range of beautiful Turkish *kilims* and carpets that you won't find elsewhere on the island.

✉ Canbulat Sokak, Keryneia ☎ 815 8413

Nakkas

Cluttered with antiques and bric-a-brac, this tiny shop offers up everything from old brass coffee pots to intricately patterned copper trays; a joy to explore.

✉ Canbulat Sokak, Keryneia ☎ 866 5571

JEWELLERY SHOPS

These can be found dotted about the streets of all the North's main towns, but a good place to shop around is on the main street of Keryneia (Girne), where several are found in a cluster around the crossroads leading down to the seafront promenade.

CULTURAL EVENTS

A variety of art exhibitions, seminars and other cultural events in the North take place throughout the year. Contact the Atatürk Kültür Merkezi (Atatürk Cultural Centre, ☎ 228 3257) or check www.whatson-northcyprus.com in Northern Nicosia for details.

SPORT

BIRDWATCHING

Ornek Holidays

Tours and tailor-made packages for small and large groups.

✉ Mete Adanic Caddesi, Keryneia ☎ 815 8969; www.ornekholidays.com

DIVING

Amphora Diving

✉ Escape Beach, Keryneia ☎ 859 24924; www.amphoradiving.com

Sight Locator Index

This index relates to the maps on the covers. We have given map references to the main sights of interest in the book. Grid references in italics indicate sights featured on the town plans. Some sights within towns may not be plotted on the maps.

Index

Acknowledgements

The Automobile Association would like to thank the following photographers, companies and picture libraries for their assistance in the preparation of this book.

Abbreviations for the picture credits are as follows: - (t) top; (b) bottom; (l) left; (r) right; (AA) AA World Travel Library.

4l Pano Panagia, AA/R Rainford; **4c** Larnaca Airport, AA/A Kouprianoff; **4r** Kyrenia, AA/A Kouprianoff; **5l** Petra tou Romiou, AA/M Birkitt; **5c** Lefkara, AA/S/L Day; **6/7** Pano Panagia, AA/R Rainford; **8/9** fishing nets, AA/A Kouprianoff; **10/1t** harbour Pafos, AA/A Kouprianoff; **10bl** Sanctuary of Apollo Hylates, AA/A Kouprianoff; **10br** man and donkey Pafos, AA/A Kouprianoff; **11** Ayios Theodhoros, AA/A Kouprianoff; **12** salad, AA/A Kouprianoff; **13t** café Pafos harbour, AA/S Day; **13c** Cyprus Delights, AA/A Kouprianoff; **12/3** fishermen Larnaka, AA/S Day; **14** wines and spirits, Larnaka, AA/R Rainford; **14/5** shop keeper, AA/A Kouprianoff; **15** grapes, AA/A Kouprianoff; **16/7** Kourion, AA/M Birkitt; **17l** Famagusta beach, AA/A Kouprianoff; **17r** wedding Xylotymbou, AA/A Kouprianoff; **18** Artemis trail, AA/A Kouprianoff; **19** Mount Olympus, AA/S Day; **20/1** Larnaca airport, AA/A Kouprianoff; **25** Greek dancers, AA/M Birkitt; **29** taxi driver, AA/A Kouprianoff; **30** public telephone, AA/M Birkitt; **31** tour bus, AA/A Kouprianoff; **34/5** Kyrenia, AA/A Kouprianoff; **36 and 36/7** St Hilarion Castle, AA/A Kouprianoff; **38** Akamas Peninsula, AA/S Day; **38/9** coastline Akamas Peninsula, AA/A Kouprianoff; **39** walkers Akamas Peninsula, AA/S Day; **40** embroidery Mevlevi Tekke, AA/M Birkitt; **40/1** Salt Lake, AA/A Kouprianoff; **41** Hala Sultan Tekke Mosque, AA/S Day; **42** Kourion, AA/M Birkitt; **42/3** Kourion, AA/R Rainford; **43** amphitheatre Kourion, AA/M Birkitt; **44** petrol tank, AA/R Rainford; **44/5** Lara, AA/S Day; **45t,c** loggerhead turtles, Lara, AA/A Kouprianoff; **46/7** Venetian wall, Nicosia, S Day; **47t** Corner of Venetian Wall, AA/A Kouprianoff; **47b** Nicosia, AA/S Day; **48tl** mosaic House of Dionysos, AA/R Rainford; **48bl** Tombs of the Kings, AA/M Birkitt; **48/9** mosaic Pafos, AA/S Day; **50/1** Kykkos Monastery, AA/S Day; **51** painting, Kykkos Monastery AA/A Kouprianoff; **52** Salamis, AA/A Kouprianoff; **52/3** Salamis, AA/A Kouprianoff; **53** mosaic Salamis, AA/A Kouprianoff; **54** Troodos foothills, AA/A Kouprianoff; **54/5** Kaledonia Falls, AA/S Day; **55** lady fruit seller, AA/M Birkitt; **56/7** Petra tou Romiou, AA/M Birkitt; **58/9** café, Latsi, AA/A Kouprianoff; **60/1** lace, Lefkara, AA/A Kouprianoff; **62/3** Amathous, AA/S Day; **64/5** hang-glider, AA/A Kouprianoff; **66** children, AA/A Kouprianoff; **68/9** Coral Bay, AA/S Day; **70** cat sculpture, Cyprus Museum, AA/M Birkitt; **71t** Museum of Folk Art, Nicosia, AA/S Day; **71b** Leda and the Swan mosaic, Cyprus Museum, AA/R Rainford; **72/3** Limassol, AA/A Kouprianoff; **73** Limassol, AA/M Birkitt; **74/5** Panagia Chrysorrogiatissa, AA/A Kouprianoff; **76/7** Hotel, Limassol, AA/A Kouprianoff; **78** Akamas Peninsular, AA/A Kouprianoff; **80/1** Turkish Nicosia, AA/A Kouprianoff; **82/3** Lefkara, AA/S Day; **85** Priest, AA/S Day; **86** Agios Lazaros church, AA/A Kouprianoff; **86/7** Larnaka, AA/M Birkitt; **88/9c** Pierides Museum, Larnaca, AA/A Kouprianoff; **88/9b** Kition, AA/A Kouprianoff; **89** Fort, Larnaka, AA/M Birkitt; **90** Agia Napa, AA/M Birkitt; **91** Hala Sultan Tekke, AA/A Kouprianoff; **92** Nissi Beach, AA/R Rainford; **92/3** Potamos, AA/S Day; **94/5** Stravrouni monastery, AA/R Rainford; **96** Stravrouni monastery, AA/A Kouprianoff; **103** Limassol, AA/M Birkitt; **105** Limassol, AA/M Birkitt; **106/7** Castle, Limassol, AA/M Birkitt; **107** Aphrodite of Soli, Cyprus Museum, AA/R Rainford; **108/9** Municipal Gardens, Limassol, AA/M Birkitt; **109** Akrotiri Peninsula, AA/A Kouprianoff; **110** Khirokitia, AA/M Birkitt; **111** Kolossi Castle, AA/A Kouprianoff; **112** Lefkara, AA/S Day; **112/3** Petra tou Romiou, AA/S Day; **114** Temple of Apollo Hylates, AA/A Kouprianoff; **121** Pafos, AA/M Birkitt; **122/3** Agia Solomoni, AA/A Kouprianoff; **124/5** Pafos, AA/M Birkitt; **125** St Paul's Pillar, AA/S Day; **126** Saranda Kolones, AA/S Day; **127** Tomb of the Kings, AA/A Kouprianoff; **128/9** Agios Neofytos monastery, AA/S Day; **130** Agia Paraskevi, AA/S Day; **131** Palaia Pafos, AA/M Birkitt; **132/3** Chrysorrogiatissa monastery, AA/A Kouprianoff; **133** Pano Panagia, AA/R Rainford; **134** Polis, AA/A Kouprianoff; **134/5** Pomos, AA/A Kouprianoff; **141** Nicosia, AA/R Rainford; **142** Archbishop Makarios statue, AA/S Day; **142/3** Agios Ionnis cathedral, AA/A Kouprianoff; **143** Agios Ionnis cathedral, AA/M Birkitt; **144** Cyprus museum, AA/R Rainford; **144/5** Cyprus museum, AA/A Kouprianoff; **145** Famagusta Gate, AA/M Birkitt; **146** Omeriye Mosque, AA/M Birkitt; **148** Buyuk Han, AA/R Bulmar; **148/9** Buyuk Han, AA/M Birkitt; **149** Turkish Cypriot lady, AA/S Day; **150** Mevlevi Tekke, AA/A Kouprianoff; **151** Selimiye Mosque, AA/A Kouprianoff; **152/3** Kakopetria, AA/M Birkitt; **154/5** Machairas Monastery, AA/M Birkitt; **155** Artemis trail, AA/A Kouprianoff; **156/7** Pedoulas, AA/S Day; **158** Panagia Tou Asinou, © Martin Mayer/Alamy; **165** Famagusta, AA/A Kouprianoff; **167** Lala Mustafa Pasa Mosque, AA/A Kouprianoff; **168/9** St George of the Latins, AA/A Kouprianoff; **169** Citadel, AA/R Bulmar; **170** St Peter and St Paul church, AA/A Kouprianoff; **170/1** Famagusta, AA/H Ulucam; **172** Bellapais Abbey, AA/A Kouprianoff; **173** Kantara castle, AA/R Bulmar; **174** Kyrenia, AA; **176/7** Soli, AA/H Ulucam; **178t** Vouni, AA; **178** Vouni, AA/A Kouprianoff.

Every effort has been made to trace the copyright holders, and we apologise in advance for any accidental errors. We would be happy to apply the corrections in the following edition of this publication.